# EXPLORING THE CASTLE

# EXPLORING THE CASTLE

DISCOVERING THE BACKBONE OF THE WORLD IN
## SOUTHERN ALBERTA

ROBERT KERSHAW

Rocky
Mountain Books
VANCOUVER • VICTORIA • CALGARY

Rocky Mountain Books
#108 – 17665 66A Avenue
Surrey, BC  V3S 2A7
www.rmbooks.com

Rocky Mountain Books
PO Box 468
Custer, WA
98240-0468

Library and Archives Canada Cataloguing in Publication

Kershaw, Robert, 1957-
    Exploring the Castle : discovering the backbone of the world in southern Alberta / Robert Kershaw.

Includes bibliographical references and index.
ISBN 978-1-897522-04-2

    1. Castle Wilderness (Alta.)  2. Natural history--Alberta--Castle Wilderness.  3. Castle Wilderness (Alta.)--History.  4. Trails--Alberta--Castle Wilderness--Guidebooks.  5. Castle Wilderness (Alta.)--Guidebooks. I. Title.

FC3695.S65K47 2008        971.23'4        C2007-907287-9

Library of Congress Control Number: 2007943345

Edited by Joe Wilderson
Cover and book design by Chyla Cardinal
Front Cover: View east from ridge above Spionkop Valley along the Front Range of the Castle.
All photographs © Robert Kershaw unless otherwise noted.

Printed and bound in Hong Kong

Rocky Mountain Books gratefully acknowledges the financial support of the Government of Canada through the Book Publishing Industry Development Program (BPIDP); the Canada Council for the Arts; and the province of British Columbia through the British Columbia Arts Council and the Book Publishing Tax Credit for our publishing activities.

This book has been produced on 100% post-consumer recycled paper, processed chlorine free and printed with vegetable-based dyes.

DISCLAIMER
The actions described within this book may be considered inherently dangerous activities. Individuals undertake these activities at their own risk. The information put forth in this guide has been collected from a variety of sources and is not guaranteed to be completely accurate or reliable. Many conditions and some information may change owing to weather and numerous other factors beyond the control of the authors and publishers. Individual climbers and/or hikers must determine the risks, use their own judgment, and take full responsibility for their actions. Do not depend on any information found in this book for your own personal safety. Your safety depends on your own good judgment based on your skills, education, and experience.
    It is up to the users of this guidebook to acquire the necessary skills for safe experiences and to exercise caution in potentially hazardous areas. The authors and publishers of this guide accept no responsibility for your actions or the results that occur from another's actions, choices, or judgments. If you have any doubt as to your safety or your ability to attempt anything described in this guidebook, do not attempt it.

# Contents

## Acknowledgements

The route this book has taken is much like hiking the Castle. With its winding, unmarked and often overgrown trails there is always the risk of getting lost. So it is two and a half years after heading out on my first hike that I have arrived in a place I had not intended to go – at least not where I thought I was heading. At times it did seem I'd lost my way, as a simple guidebook was turning into a monstrous undertaking. I realize now this was not the case. What was discovered was meant to be. The rewards of finding my own path into the Castle and discovering the backbone of the world were worth the risk of getting lost.

Then again it wasn't just my journey alone. I owe the origins of this book to the friends who shared many trails along the way, not just over the past two years but throughout my 12 years living in the shadow of the Castle – notably David McNeill, who gave me my first job as a writer in the area but eventually became a dear friend and my most reliable hiking companion; Michael Gerrand, whose love of the Front Range is infectious and who knows a thing or two about weeds and native grasses; Phil Hazelton, who has always made his home in the Gladstone Valley my home; Hilah Simmons, who can find the greatest pleasure in the simplest of things; Deb Simmons, who has always encouraged me to take the necessary risks; Ken Williams and all my Buffalo Runner brothers and sisters; Heather Devine, whose knowledge of history and brilliant mind stirred me to do better; Karsten, Leanne and Zev for following their passions and for bringing us with them on their necessary journeys, and Karsten again for being the first to review and critique my manuscript; Lorne Fitch for his aerial photographs; Farley Wuth for providing access to the Kootenai Brown Pioneer Museum's wonderful archives; and all the writers and advocates for wilderness who continue to inspire me. Words can't truly thank the Main family – especially Janet, Cas and Mac – who opened a door for me onto this landscape, a door that will never, ever close; and thank you, Janet, for your unwavering strength and generosity. You taught me to live with kindness and dignity no matter the obstacles.

I would also like to thank the organizations and individuals who contributed to this book – Canadian Parks and Society Wilderness Calgary/

Banff Chapter, TD Friends of the Environment (Calgary Chapter), The Wilburforce Foundation, Nelson Arthur Hyland Foundation, Stella Thompson and the Castle-Crown Wilderness Coalition, and a special thanks to Don Gorman of Rocky Mountain Books for believing in the project and keeping me on his radar when deadlines were missed. Of course this book would truly never have happened without my good friend Joe Obad. Joe had the thankless and conflicting roles of chief ally and obligatory foil. Many hours were spent arguing over ideas and language. Somehow Joe never lost his sense of humour or his trust in me. The book is simply better because of Joe's unrivalled commitment to it and more importantly to the Castle.

Finally I thank my family, who mean the world to me, and to Emily's family who have made it that much bigger and brighter. And of course to Emily, whose love got me back to the trailhead.

—Robert Kershaw

**Acknowledgements from Canadian Parks & Wilderness Society**
The Canadian Parks & Wilderness Society (cpaws) has, along with several other organizations, urged for the protection of the Castle Wilderness for decades. When the idea of a guide was first discussed with Robert Kershaw we knew he would require a lot of support. Cpaws is proud to have assisted Rob in producing this excellent guide to help you explore and understand the Castle. Our assistance, however, was based on the generosity of other organizations and individuals who provided resources to this project. Particular thanks are due to the TD Friends of the Environment (Calgary Chapter), The Wilburforce Foundation, Nelson Arthur Hyland Foundation, Stella Thompson and the Castle-Crown Wilderness Coalition and donations made by friends and colleagues of Jim Leslie, in memory of a true lover of the Canadian Rockies. Thanks goes to Rocky Mountain Books, who believed in this project and helped usher Rob and cpaws through the publishing process of creating a guidebook. Special thanks go to rmb's Don Gorman for his vision, persistence and rigour.

The greatest appreciation is saved for the author himself, Robert Kershaw. In supporting this project, CPAWS hoped to spread appreciation and concern for the Castle by providing a credible writer from the region a chance to explore the Castle in guidebook form. We believe readers will find in Rob's writing much of what is admirable in him as a person. He's a friend of the land, an insightful philosopher on cultural and natural history, and a provocative questioner – inquiring about what has taken place, what's happening now and what may happen in the future of the Castle region – just the sort of person you'd like to hike with. The next best thing is this book, into which he has poured much of his life and passion. Keep it with you in the Castle and, like time spent with Rob, you'll be richer for the experience. For all his efforts here CPAWS expresses our heartfelt, abiding gratitude to Rob for the hundreds of hours of effort he has put into *Exploring the Castle: Discovering the Backbone of the World.* For news about the Castle and information on how you can help protect the area, please visit www.cpawscalgary.org.

Joe Obad
Conservation Director – SW Alberta
Canadian Parks & Wilderness Society,
Calgary/Banff Chapter

Wilburforce
*foundation*

Friends of the Environment Foundation

CANADIAN PARKS AND WILDERNESS SOCIETY
CALGARY/BANFF CHAPTER

*To Em, my backbone.*

# Discovering the Backbone of the World

# Introduction/Preface

> *"So long as human consciousness remains within the hills, canyons, cliffs and the plants, animals and sky, the term landscape as it has entered the English language is misleading. A portion of territory the eye can comprehend in a single view does not correctly describe the relationship between a human being and his or her surroundings."*
>
> —Leslie Marmon Silko

Not long after I moved into an old homestead along Yarrow Creek on the eastern edge of the Castle in 1994 I was hired to research and write the material for a recreational trail map of southwest Alberta. For a naive exile from the city it was a welcome opportunity to explore the very landscape that had lured me down here in the first place.

The map covered an area from the Oldman River south to the United States border and from the Continental Divide east to Highway 2. To its credit it profiled most of the trails and all the recreational activities the region had to offer. The map, however, was not without its concerns. The scale was too grand and its "origami" awkward. As well, some of the information was inaccurate or has since become outdated. Regrettably it merely gave cursory descriptions of the area's unique climate, landforms, plants and animals and barely skimmed the essential natural and cultural histories. Of consequence the map promoted an 'anything goes' recreational perspective, a point of view that has consequences for the future of the Castle. When discussing the possibility of a new guidebook with friends it was clear that whatever came about it would have to be oriented differently.

Ten years later I returned to the Castle and over the course of that summer and fall hiked and documented 22 trails through the Front Range canyons, the South and West Castle valleys and the Carbondale River drainage. Sometimes I was accompanied by friends more knowledgeable about the region. Other times I was joined by acquaintances from further away who were excited to be experiencing the Castle for the first time. Most of the time, however, I hiked solo. Regardless with whom or how many, the experience was profound. Revisiting past hikes while discovering new ones refuelled a passion for the Castle and the surrounding region that had flatlined over the past few years.

Compared to other popular mountain park areas, the Castle's valleys and ridges see relatively few hikers. But the Castle is not empty of humans by any means. It has a long history, at least 350 generations, of sustained and managed land use – timber for tipis, stone for tools, plants for medicines, wildlife for food and clothing. Today the demands on the Castle are of a

View from old Main family homestead
looking out to Front Range of the Castle.

different scale and attitude. Earth is excavated, grass grazed, timber felled, wells drilled, trophies hunted, trails manoeuvred and mountains scaled. Each of these uses offers a limited individual perception at the expense of a collective awareness. To one person the bank along a mountain stream is a place to experience the Castle's natural beauty. To someone else it is the buffer zone for a nearby clearcut. To another it is a site to research plants or animals, and to yet another it is merely an obstacle to be negotiated on their all-terrain vehicle.

There is no denying that continued resource extraction, unregulated long-term camping, and heavy motorized trail use are damaging the Castle's critical natural and historical features. One visit can leave you with the feeling that the land and water are being used to death. Even those of us who take to trails on foot contribute to the impact. Experts agree that protecting the Castle is key to keeping the larger Crown of the Continent ecosystem intact. But what does this mean and who are the experts? Wildlife habitat protection is critical to good land use decisions. Often, innovative concepts of conservation biology are ignored by government policies. But science and politics only tell us part of the Castle's story. As we continue to rely on biologists and governments to rehabilitate and manage the places we care for, we must also begin to acknowledge the importance of settlement, land use and the stories of ordinary experience. These narratives offer an untapped resource for understanding the complicated, shifting connection between human behaviour and the land. Without these stories a language capable of conveying some of the most essential qualities of the Castle is being lost.

To those accepting and willing, this book offers an overview – a brief narrative history, really – of the Castle and surrounding landscape. It is also a trail guide with maps, photos and descriptions explaining where, when and how to enjoy the Castle with insight and care. In its attempt to describe an entire region over so few pages the book necessarily takes liberties and leaves omissions 'on the editing floor.' Hopefully I've accomplished this tricky task with some clarity and respect. The book does not contain every possible route or historic arc. What it does offer, hopefully, is an invitation to experience a place of remarkable physical, biological, historical and cultural diversity with renewed sensitivity and awareness.

## The Castle: Still a Wild Place

*"You cannot take care of what you cannot see."*

— Dr. Gerould Wilhelm (quoted in Savage)

It was just my fourth hike of the summer. I'd chosen Three Lakes Ridge. It is a somewhat obscure route and not one of the readily hiked trails in the Castle. The trailhead off the West Castle River Valley road is not marked. The trail is often thick with alder and at times hard to follow – a grateful testament to the lack of all-terrain vehicles that roar elsewhere in the Castle.

Logistics and conditions aside, maybe it is the false promise of three alpine lakes lined up in a row along the base of the Continental Divide that keeps hikers away. But then again how would one know that the lakes really are there, only spread far apart and not exactly connected to the same ridge, if she didn't go? And what of the pleasure of the yet to be discovered: the bloom of creamy beargrass, the one readily accessible lake tightly tucked between thick forest and steep scree, the glorious view from the ridge down into the Flathead Valley, and the resident mountain goats shifting sure-footed on the precarious ledges of Scarpe Mountain. I know all this because I had hiked Three Lakes Ridge, or Rainy Lakes as it is known, eight years ago. Back then I was uncertain of my destination and graciously rewarded. This time I was more assured. The day started out full of promises to be kept.

Despite the sunshine and my eager anticipation, however, I found I could not fully relax. Bears had been on my mind as I approached my summer of hiking the Castle. Grizzlies and black bears are part of the fabric. I knew this. I'd seen bears here and elsewhere in the past. There was the black bear sow and her two young cubs that I met back in 1997. I still like to imagine my harmonica playing set the mother at ease before she quietly and matter-of-factly led her family off the trail just in front of me. Then there was the grizzly bear I watched one hot summer day as he ambled out of the trees and into Crandell Lake in Waterton Lakes National Park. He swam out 50 yards, swam back, shook himself and left. There was also the incredible experience of seeing a dozen black bears during a two-day river trip in the Northwest Territories. But these experiences were all some time ago. My more recent bear sightings had been from the safety of a vehicle at garbage dumps in the northern communities where I was working. Dump runs and bear sightings were a form of entertainment, a way to ward off boredom. Wildness and boredom: no two states of mind could be further apart.

Now back in the Castle, bears were on my mind again and my keenness was waning. As I continued up the trail, sights and sounds were less familiar. The trail was less open, wilder than I remembered. By the time I got to the old logged clearing below the first basin, dark clouds had rolled in and all familiarity was gone. It was eerily quiet with not a breath of wind. My earlier casual uneasiness was now edgy and hard. And then, true to the trail's more familiar name, it began to rain.

More common west of the Continental Divide, beargrass, with its creamy, torch-like cluster of flowers, blooms throughout the subalpine.

Discovering the Backbone of the World

A dozen routes through the clearing offered themselves to me. Which to take? I continued along what seemed the most obvious trail, but it did not offer a way up into the basin. I should have taken the forest trail, the one that followed along the edge of the clearing. But I failed to remember this. The rain came heavy now. Even the torch-like brilliance of beargrass throughout the valley was intimidating. I felt exposed and vulnerable as I circled around trying to decide whether to wait out the rain or turn around and go home. It was then I saw the biggest pile of bear scat of my life, grizzly, maybe a few hours old, maybe less, difficult to say in the cooling rain. I spooked and quickly turned in my tracks and left. No longer connected to my surroundings, I bristled with every rustle from the bushes. Back at the trailhead I retrieved my stashed mountain bike and with the day's promises left undelivered on the high ridge, pedalled hard back to my car. By Beaver Mines the rain had stopped and the sun was shining once again.

It wasn't the Castle that repelled me back down the trail. The trail had only offered what it had to give and what I had asked of it even though I wasn't quite ready to accept it: a wild experience. The Castle would offer much over the course of the months to come. I would experience bear sightings on later hikes and would marvel at them. I would also eventually return to Three Lakes and summit the ridge.

## Why the Castle Matters

> *It is difficult to comprehend a landscape that at first glance holds little distinction. Why explore this Castle and not Castle Junction, the more famous mountain landscape with the same regal name? Why seek out the lesser-known wilderness?*
>
> — Journal entry, July 2005

Driving down Highway 22, which is one of the primary routes into the southwest corner of Alberta, you become increasingly aware of a region different from the celebrity of Banff and Jasper National Parks. A rolling mosaic of ranchland, Douglas-fir- and limber-pine-crested ridges – and a line of peaks different and more inviting than the steely, limestone massifs of Kananaskis Country – begins to emerge. Almost nowhere else in North America can you see such intimacy between mountains and prairie. From all directions leading into the Castle, whether from Alberta, Montana or British Columbia, highways and railways intersect rivers and cross mountain passes; dusty roads traverse expanses of grassland pasture, drop down into cottonwood-choked coulees and wind around dome-shaped buttes. Small towns live and die at the crossroads. The Piikani, Kainai and Ktunaxa Nations persevere, their present-day reserves and territories mere remnants of a rich, expansive history. Comparisons between mountain regions are not usually justifiable, but the impression upon entering Castle country is one of discovering a very special place.

Windsor Mountain seen from Victoria Ridge. The Castle is an ancient and diverse landscape that has supported humans for thousands of years, and plants and animals for hundreds of thousands of years more.

The Castle is approximately a quarter of a million acres (1040 square kilometres) of Alberta Forest Reserve public land within the Municipality of Pincher Creek, bordered by the Flathead Provincial Forest, the Municipality of Crowsnest Pass and Waterton Lakes National Park. Designated within Alberta's C5 Forest Reserve as the Castle Special Management Area Forest Land Use Zone, the Castle is managed under the provincial government's Sustainable Resource Development Department. But unless one is familiar with the meanings and policies behind the official wording, these designations tell us little.

More telling is that the Castle is an integral part of the Oldman River Basin and the Rocky Mountain Cordillera. It is an ancient and diverse landscape that has supported humans for thousands of years, and plants and animals for hundreds of thousands of years more. It is a refuge for deer, elk, mountain sheep and goat that rises quickly from the eastern grasslands, through valleys, over ridges and onward to its 2600-metre peaks along the Continental Divide. This is a vital region of deep valleys and accessible alpine passes that provide passageways for large carnivores so they can follow their prey without end north and south through the Clark and Flathead ranges. A broad assortment of habitats support a marvellous mixture of trees, shrubs, wildflowers, grasses, ferns, sedges and lichens. Over half the flora species in Alberta are represented here – an estimated 824 different vascular plants, 160 of them rare provincially and 38 that are rare nationally – as well as some of the largest and last intact montane forest in the province.

The Castle is also an integral part of a human landscape that reaches far beyond its boundaries. In a fleeting act of restraint the region's major rivers – the South Castle, West Castle and Carbondale – together with their tributaries and numerous high-elevation lakes absorb more snow and rain than almost anywhere else in Alberta. The significance of this water storehouse often goes unheralded. While it makes up only 5 per cent of the Oldman River Basin's vast six million acres, the Castle's watersheds and sub-basins contribute upwards of 30 per cent of the water needed to keep the arid ranchland, farmland and thirsty towns downstream thriving.

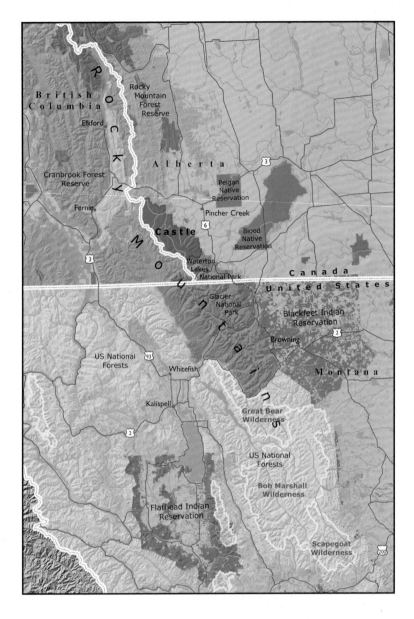

The Castle is approximately a quarter of a million acres (1040 km²) of Alberta Forest Reserve public land in the southwesternmost corner of Alberta.

Despite official and unofficial recognition of its 'specialness,' however, the Castle remains contentious. Local, provincial and national organizations continue to fight for legal protection of the place under the evocative banner of 'the Castle Wilderness.' Other voices argue for the continued removal of natural resources and unrestricted use of the region's roads and trails. To date, the latter groups hold the upper hand.

It seems that prescribed designations, and even the innocent view from a roadside turnout, only go so far in describing a place, let alone conserving it. Official designations tend to simplify the area's rich and varied histories, and the roadside view takes little notice of local connections to the land. Missing in our descriptions and designations are the voices and sounds of cultures and creatures whose lives are often worn down or destroyed by contending political forces. To understand the power of the land, to care for it, to reimagine it as a wilder place, we have to walk it, ride its rivers, listen to and tell its stories.

### Lifting the Crown to Find the Backbone

*"Many landscape features that initially seem identical in our eyes to landforms we've seen elsewhere turn out, on close examination, to be unique to a place."*

— Barry Lopez, *Home Ground*

From 1995 through 1997 I co-owned and published the *Waterton-Glacier Views*, a weekly summer newspaper that covered southwestern Alberta and northwestern Montana. It was an ambitious, some might say foolish, undertaking. Every week from late spring to early fall David McNeill and I would gather and write stories from in and around the Waterton-Glacier International Peace Park. Dave, a news junkie and the more experienced writer, contributed and edited most of the stories. I was in charge of layout and production but had commissioned myself to write a weekly column, something you can do when you own your own publication. I called the feature "Road Songs: Travelling with the *Waterton-Glacier Views*." Every week I would take to the highway and deliver the news.

The route was an exhausting 800-kilometre marathon that circumnavigated Waterton Lakes and Glacier national parks. From dawn to dusk I dropped off upwards of 10,000 newspapers in the surrounding communities: Pincher Creek, Blairmore, Coleman, Bellevue, Frank, Hillcrest, Fort Macleod, Cardston, Hill Spring, Twin Butte, Waterton, Babb, Browning, St. Mary's, East Glacier, West Glacier and Kalispell. As the sun set I would return against the grain over the Going-to-the-Sun Road, desperate to make the Chief Mountain border crossing before it closed.

Despite the long haul it was a welcome respite from storylines and deadlines. Once a week I was able to roll down the car window and breathe in, if only for fleeting moments, the expanse of grassland, forests and mountains that had compelled me to move to southern Alberta in the first place. I also met and talked to all sorts of people – visitors and residents alike – a cultural diversity obscured by the more popular myths of cowboys and Indians. For that one day I was both alone and in the best

Yarrow Creek flows out from the mountains along the eastern edge of the Castle.

of company. It was through these weekly drives that I began to appreciate a broader, deeper landscape. But it was only a beginning. I had yet to discover the significance of what and who had come before.

It was a landscape that conservationist and author George Bird Grinnell also came to appreciate in the late 19th century. During a trip through what would become Glacier National Park Grinnell took note of a network of mountains, valleys, lakes and rivers on either side of the Continental Divide as far as the eye could see. From a vantage point in this mountain wilderness, water flows in three directions: north to Hudson's Bay, south to the Gulf of Mexico and west to the Pacific. Millions of years of geological upheaval, the advances and retreats of snow and ice, floods and droughts, and more than 10,000 years of human collaboration and conflict has resulted in a land with a unique temperament. Grinnell was obviously inspired by this majestic land and the people and wildlife it sustained. Disregarding political boundaries, he named it "The Crown of the Continent." But the roots go deeper.

While Grinnell's designation speaks dramatically of the region's splendour, it does so with more than a passing nod to European monarchy, colonialism and scientific discovery. Crown of the Continent is a name entrenched in its own historical conceit and not in the way of life that existed long before European dominance. The Blackfoot called the expanse of mountains and valleys *Mo'kakiikin* – "backbone of the world."[1] The Blackfoot didn't need a mountaintop view to comprehend 480,000 square kilometres of ragged Rocky Mountain spine, the importance of the many cultures that live in its shadow, the myriad plants and animals that inhabit every possible niche from grassland to alpine, and all the essential rivers that flow from its hundreds of watersheds, supplying almost 25 per cent of North America's fresh water (Ferguson, 30). Indigenous peoples like the Blackfoot took note of territory through actions and words, not fences and land-title deeds. Place names linked them to the land through stories passed down through generations in a way that was more than just functional or descriptive. Place names and stories rooted them to a *meaning* of place.

---

1         According to Anthropologist Eldon Yellowhorn, "the Rocky Mountains, *Mo'kakiikin*, were known collectively as the 'backbone of the world.'" The Blackfoot word 'miistakis' has also been used to refer to 'backbone of the world' but actually only translates as 'mountains.'

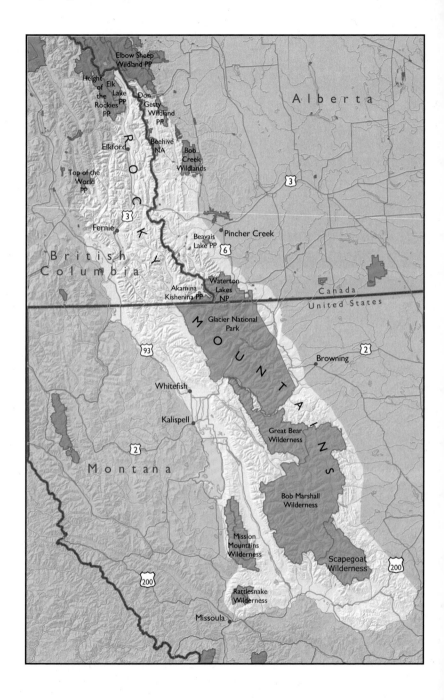

Two hundred years ago, and only one hundred before Grinnell's "discovery," *Mo'kakiikin* stories were unknown. To future colonists the prairies and mountains were simply, as Irene Spry put it, "a wild, sparsely peopled waste." The westernmost edge of European narrative was a remote trading post at the junction of the Red Deer and South Saskatchewan rivers, just east of today's Alberta/Saskatchewan boundary, where only the tiny settlement of Estuary and a ferry crossing the South Saskatchewan remain. Three centuries of European exploration of North America had barely penetrated the northwestern plains, let alone the northern Rocky Mountains and the Castle. What knowledge the European traders possessed came from the region's indigenous peoples – the Ktunaxa, the Siksika, the Kainai, the Piikani, among many. Various clans and coalitions had spread out over the Plains for thousands of years. They travelled the Rocky Mountain Front on foot from the Yukon to Mexico, traversed the mountain passes, crossed the Divide, hunted, fished, trapped, traded, shared knowledge and ceremonies, and clashed to defend territory.

Today the term Crown of the Continent means something else again. Scientists and a growing community of local conservationists recognize the region as one of the largest and most important ecologically intact areas in North America, covering over 10.3 million acres from the Bob Marshall wilderness area north to the Highwood River. Larger than Vancouver Island by a third, and 60 per cent of it public land, the Castle is an ecosystem largely defined by its diverse habitat and wildlife species that range north and south, east and west. In the context of conservation biology the Crown of the Continent can still evoke the promise of a connected landscape despite being divided by national and provincial borders and managed under an assortment of governmental jurisdictions and mandates. But the notion of *Mo'kakiikin*, of a connected landscape of human experience and spirit, still remains a footnote for most.

Alberta Portion of the Crown of the
Continent Ecosystem Showing the Castle.
Map created by the Miistakis Institute, published
courtesy of the Canadian Parks & Wilderness Society.

## Going to the Far Outside

*How can you tell the story of the Castle in which the land isn't a*
*character?*

— Journal entry, October 2005

Stories about the western landscape flourish. Many are written about the
greater Rocky Mountain Cordillera or specific regions closely associated
with the Castle. Peter Douglas Elias, in his informative book *From Grass-*
*lands to Rockland: An Explorer's Guide to the Ecosystems of Southernmost Al-*
*berta*, begins with Captain John Palliser's 1857 expedition before describing
the various scientific land classifications and the more dramatic forces of
natural history. Ralph Waldt, in his striking *Crown of the Continent: The Last*
*Great Wilderness of the Rocky Mountains*, leads us with a naturalist's keen
awareness and the solitary photographer's lens into a wild and colourful
landscape. Frank Clifford, in *The Backbone of the World: A Portrait of the Van-*
*ishing West along the Continental Divide*, chooses to follow the path of the
rugged individualists along the Continental Divide, iconoclasts that stand
firm in "a harsh, unforgiving region." All these authors love the land they
write about, and each book is an important contribution to our understanding of wilderness areas like the Castle and why they matter.

We still like to classify western wilderness and define our experiences
there through the lens of modern environmental science or stories of
exploration and adventure. Most guidebooks and natural histories continue
to be oriented this way. But as Arizona ethnobotanist Gary Paul Nabhan
reasons: "The plants and animals ... hardly seem to be waiting for me to
give them meaning." I also suspect Nabhan would rather reveal the more
unheralded histories, the shared community rituals and practices that inform
the places we live in or travel through than any chosen individual's heroic
actions. He offers a different route to knowing a place – more narrative
path than information highway, more nuance than data – what he describes
as *the naturalist's trance*: "the hunter's pursuit of wild game, the curandera's
search for hidden roots, the fisherman's casting of the net into the current,
the water witcher's trust of the forked willow branch, the rock climber's

fixation on the slightest details of a cliff face." It is a humanist approach to wild places, one that is capricious and absolutely includes people.

So I'll take a new path into the Castle, twisting through time and place, and begin with a story about a map.

## Ac ko Mok ki's Map

In the winter of 1801, Blackfoot chief Ac ko Mok ki drew a map for Peter Fidler, a Welsh surveyor for the Hudson's Bay Company. Frontiersmen like Fidler relied heavily on the knowledge and experience of the Blackfoot and other indigenous peoples on the prairies and in the mountains as they sought to extend the Company's trading empire westward.[2] With considerable detail and sophistication, Ac ko Mok ki's map introduced Fidler to an area of 320,000 square kilometres, half the size of Alberta, from the junction of the Yellowstone and Missouri rivers across the Rocky Mountains to the Pacific Ocean. It also showed the locations of 32 cultural groups as well as their populations. Instead of virgin land, the map portrayed an existing network of civilization and trade throughout the northwest plains and beyond.

What is so strikingly different from a contemporary cartographic point of view is the position of the mountains and their relationship to the rivers. The mountains, shown as a double line, run horizontally along the top of the map, not unlike a backbone supporting the belly of the land. It is rivers, however, that truly define the map. Thirteen rivers, each one named and leading out of its respective mountain valley, are drawn in a symmetrical array like arteries or, better still, nerves, toward the Missouri River running down the centre of the map. Above the mountains, two rivers flow off the page to the Pacific Ocean. And to the far right, three more rivers, including the Oldman, flow out of the mountains toward Hudson Bay. One might well imagine what Fidler thought as he looked the map over. He had been guided near these mountains once before, even crossed the Oldman River, but never could he have imagined such a vast

---

2        It is believed that as early as 1807 Ktunaxa guides had drawn a map for David Thompson that included the peoples and territories all the way to the west coast.

area offering so many potential trade routes and trading partners. He was indeed looking into the future through the past.

Ac ko Mok ki's map eventually made it to the drawing table of British cartographer Aaron Arrowsmith. In 1802 Arrowsmith used this fresh perspective to fill in the large blank space that had occupied his previous map of the North American interior. Arrowsmith called his map *A Map Exhibiting All the New Discoveries in the Interior Parts of North America*. The matter of accurately mapping the West and staking claim was crucial in the race for territorial control. Now a map showing places that would eventually become Alberta, Saskatchewan, Wyoming and Montana was in the hands of both the British and the American governments. In 1804 President Thomas Jefferson commissioned Lewis and Clark to follow the route first described by Ac ko Mok ki up the Missouri River. Until Lewis and Clark's map was published, in 1814, Ac ko Mok ki's map remained the most accurate map of the region (Warhus, 154–158).

The fate of Ac ko Mok ki's map is a telling example of the appropriation and transformation of an indigenous landscape. At a time when the

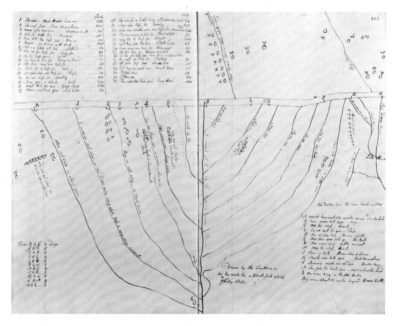

## Ac ko Mok ki

Ac ko Mok ki was the son of the famed Siksika chief of the same name. The elder Ac ko Mok ki (Old Swan) was possibly the most influential Blackfoot leader during the 1780s and '90s and was, according to frontiersman Duncan McGillvery, "respected and esteemed by all the neighbouring tribes" (Binnema, 175). After Ac ko Mok ki senior died in 1794, his son assumed his name and tried to keep the peace among the Blackfoot, Cree, Assiniboine and the Europeans. The fragile harmony finally came to an end 12 years later, when, with the aid of Ac ko Mok ki's map, European traders and trappers began to advance deeper into the region and start new trade alliances that shifted allegiances and ultimately the balance of power. As Lewis and Clark were venturing up the Missouri and onward to the Rocky Mountains a new era in the West was taking shape.

Ac ko Mok ki's (Old Swan's) Map of 1801 from Peter Fidler's "Journal of Exploration and Survey, 1789–1804." [Hudson's Bay Co. Archives, Archives of Manitoba, E.3/2, fols. 106d-7]

Blackfoot were the dominant force in the region and the bison were still many, Ac ko Mok ki would have sketched the map out on the ground, in the sand or snow alongside a river, or in the cooling ashes of a fire. All the details would have been drawn out through his oral tradition, details from the stories of trips he had taken or trips recounted to him by others upon their return. Here, inscribed into prairie earth more than 50 years before John Palliser's expedition marched into southern Alberta and Thomas Blakiston became the first *documented* explorer to cross through the Castle and over the Divide, was a map derived from centuries of experience on the land. Fortunately or unfortunately, depending on how one views recent history, Fidler quickly copied Ac ko Mok ki's map into his journal before the next snowfall or stiff breeze erased the original forever.

Knowing the story of Ac ko Mok ki's map, we cannot help but think differently of the Castle and the landscape of which it is an integral part. It establishes a world before European contact, before the balance of power shifted, before the Crown of the Continent existed in Grinnell's Western consciousness and before wilderness needed protection. Ac ko Mok ki's story also brings us back closer in time and place to when the land took shape, back to a new beginning.

## Building Ac ko Mok ki's World

*"Nothing lasts long under the same form. I have seen what was once solid earth change into sea, and lands created out of what once was ocean. Seashells lie far away from ocean waves, and ancient anchors have been found on mountaintops."*
— Ovid, *Metamorphoses*, Book XV, 371

*Under our feet the raised beds of ancient seas remind us that we only came here yesterday*
— Sid Marty, "Mountains," from *Sky Humour*

From atop the high ridges along the Continental Divide, looking across rocky peaks and down into deep, forested valleys contemplating a continent once flat and often under water is a bit of a stretch. Along the eastern edge of the Castle, on the other hand, only minor contemplation is necessary. Here an easterly shove from deep below the earth's surface brings the mountains ever closer to the edge of the grasslands that were once an

### Peter Fidler

In 1792, the Hudson's Bay Company dispatched Peter Fidler to the prairies. A contemporary and rival of North West Company surveyor David Thompson, Fidler oversaw the building of many HBC trading posts that sprang up in the northwest plains during the late 1700s and early 1800s. Known for his relationships with Blackfoot trading parties, in particular with the local Piikani, Fidler travelled throughout southern Alberta decades before Palliser's expedition. He is also considered to be the first European to come in contact with the Ktunaxa.

30

ancient sea. It's the closest the northern Rockies come to the short-grass prairies. There are no true foothills here, a topographical omission that gives rise to the fitting but worn-out expression "from prairie grass to mountain pass."

More than a clichéd slogan for tourist brochures, this sloping lowland to highland relationship is one of the truly remarkable qualities of the Castle. It is key to the region's beginnings, to its topography, to the plants, animals and people who came to live here. The Rocky Mountain Front can be imagined, as environmental historian Dan Flores suggests, as "the viscera of the West." To go up any of the Front Range valleys – Yarwood, Spionkop, Drywood or Pincher Creek – is to seek a deeper connection to a landscape that a billion years ago was fresh and raw.

Looking southeast from Prairie Bluff to Chief Mountain. Along the eastern edge of the Castle it is possible to imagine a land that was once flat and under water.

Many of the region's cultures tell of their Creator sculpting the land with the mud brought up from the depths of a great sea by animals – a turtle, a muskrat – or of landforms surfacing like pieces of a mythical puzzle from the spirit world. Modern geology describes what was at first a relatively uninspired landscape, a three-billion-year-old rolling rock foundation, a continent without steep mountains or deep canyons to repel or retain a rising sea. When the waters flooded, what exposed rock there was eroded and settled on the seafloor. What little life survived existed near the bottom of this watery world.

As this new land materialized, wind and waves tore at the exposed formations. Particle by particle, layer by layer, sediments, small decaying invertebrates and plants washed into the sea. With each ebb and flow the

Evidence of a past, watery existence, the folds of an ancient seabed, fossilized ripples and salt crystal casts can be found high in the Castle alpine, especially along Front Range ridges like this view from Victoria Ridge.

sediment piled up. The sea became shallower and increasingly richer with life, transforming an emergent land into a muddy foundation that would eventually become known as the Great Plains. But the sculpting of the land did not stop there. It would take the casting of a stone and further geological impulses for the Rocky Mountains to emerge.

## Building the Backbone

> *"The origin of mountains had always been a topic of speculation. Genesis does not mention them at all until the story of the Flood. To many ... this meant, like tapeworms, they weren't part of the original plan."*
>
> — Alan Cutler, *The Seashell on the Mountaintop*

> *If one feature defines the Castle both physically and spiritually, it is the mountains. The Castle's peaks seductively draw your eye from afar with their soft, unique shades of purple, red and green. From in close they are less than sympathetic. Their jagged ridges, sheer cliffs, swirling winds and tumbling snow can deliver a chilling reprimand.*
>
> — Journal entry, August 2005

While the prairies suggest persistence, mountains offer escape. More than rock and ice, mountains are landscapes of desire and destiny, or what essayist Rebecca Solnit describes as "arrival and triumph."

Mountains were certainly what drew me to the region in the first place – at least their physical authority did with their unique shades of soft purples, reds and greens and waiting vistas. I would routinely head into the Castle alone or with friends, always with an elevated destination in mind. Usually we would achieve what we'd set out to do: scramble to the top of Victoria's rock-strewn peak, traverse Whistler's windswept crest or ski down a snow-choked bowl off Haig Ridge. But not always. Triumph in the mountains is unpredictable. In close, mountains are less compassionate. Their jagged ridges, sheer cliffs, swirling winds and tumbling snow can deliver sharp reprimands. While a mountain's physical presence is hard and fast, at least in human space and time, any notion of its spiritual qualities appear ghost-like and impulsive.

It is disappointing, then, that mountains typically have their origins prescribed to us only in measured quantities of geological time, plate tectonics and rock types. Young Blackfoot warriors or Ktunaxa hunters did not set foot in the Front Ranges to commune with the "Purcell Supergroup Formation." Neither did more recent alpinists scale the peaks of the Continental Divide seeking proof of "diastrophic tectonic forces." Rather, they sought dream beds high on the rocky plateaus, tracked game or pursued fresh routes up snowy cirques where they could renew their faith and test their mental and physical resolve. Today, standing in the midst of these mountains and scaling them have helped us redefine our relationship to an archetypal landform that was once considered in western religion as a pagan haunt, "an upshot of Adam and Eve's fall from grace," as Dan Flores put it.

The gothic peaks of Mount Pengelly loom over North Goat Creek headwaters. More than rock and ice, mountains are landscapes of desire and destiny.

Percy Bullchild, in *The Sun Came Down*, tells a story about a boy and a small rock cast from his pouch under orders from Creator Sun to impede the boy's evil mother. When the rock hit the ground, "A mighty range sprang up. As far as the eyes could see, in either direction, north and south, there seemed to be no end to this mysteriously placed mountain range." Blocked by the mountains, the mother runs up and down the rocky spine before eventually realizing she must either go through the mountains or over them. After getting her bearings she heads up a canyon, going as far as she can before climbing the high canyon walls. Eventually she makes it to the top. Going down the other side was just as hard, but by this time she had caught on to the rhythm and spirit of mountain climbing. "It was long hard work to get over these darn mountains Creator Sun put there as an obstacle for her, to slow her down. But soon she was back in open country and away she went." If climbing up and down the mountains made her tired, she didn't act like it.

But whether they are the result of a rock tossed unknowingly by a child or nothing more complicated than displaced dirt after some supreme force scooped out the oceans, understanding how these mountains got here in the first place holds consequences, both for those who venture into them and for those who benefit from their virtues from a distance.

Long before human pilgrimage and adventure, 75 million years ago, deep beneath the earth's Precambrian mantle, the powers that be were preparing to build the Rocky Mountains by distorting and dislocating hundreds of millions of years of sedimentary buildup. From the Yukon to the Yucatan, compressive forces under tremendous heat began to push the older sedimentary foundation up over younger formations along the Rocky Mountain Cordillera, a snub to the "old on the bottom, new on the top" rule of thumb.

Known matter-of-factly as the North American Overthrust Belt, the Clark and the Flathead ranges that pass through the Castle and the other ranges in the Crown of the Continent were part of this massive rock revival. Rock once restrained west of the Flathead Valley released its stresses and began a monumental shift. As it warped and buckled, the rock reached a breaking point and fractured. Like any clean break, one piece goes one way while another goes in the opposite direction. For one section of the crust there was no place to go but up. From Mount Kidd in the Kananaskis Valley through northern Montana, the Lewis Overthrust shoved mountainous rock as much as 100 kilometres to the east.

Compared to the Kananaskis mountains, however, the rock here in the Castle offers a further shift. Somewhere south of Beaver Mines, west of Pincher Creek, the Lewis Thrust Fault sliced deeper into the sedimentary layers, forcing the oldest of formations to rise to the surface. From the easternmost slopes of the Front Range to the Continental Divide, the Castle is considered to have among the best-preserved Precambrian sedimentary rocks in the world, well over a billion years old. To the north, such rock is not seen at the surface. In the Castle it is possible to step back over time between geological eras millions of years apart.

> *I'm lucky enough to live in the beautiful landscape of Gladstone Valley, three days' walk north of Waterton Lakes National Park. We have that technicolor view of Corner Mountain (or Prairie Bluff), Victoria Peak, Gladstone Mountain and Table Mountain right out the kitchen window to the south. When I get out into that landscape I get a whole different perspective of it. The most mind-boggling experience is to climb over the Lewis Fault, where I can stand with one foot on rock that formed a hundred million years ago or so and the other foot on rock that was created over a billion years ago ...*
>
> — Hilah Simmons in "Levitating Landscapes,"
> *Waterton Glacier Views*, 1997

But the story of the Castle's mountains does not end with this reversal of fortunes. Coinciding with the topsy-turvy strata, the mountain spine takes an odd turn to the east. For most of its length the leading edge of the Eastern Slopes of the Rockies follows a steady

## Other Geological Colourings

Red, green and grey mudstones, called argillites, found on ridges throughout the Castle, especially in the Front Range canyons; pink granites on Willoughby Ridge; and arrays of bright lichen colonies add colours not found among the grey Paleozoic limestone mountains to the north. Largely missing in the Castle are igneous rocks. Sandwiched in the Precambrian sediments is a layer of dark green basalt, known as the Purcell Lava. Drywood Creek is also a place to see this geological formation.

northwest to southeast line. This all changes 10 kilometres or so south of Beaver Mines, about the same place where the Lewis Fault cuts deepest into the Castle's Precambrian armour.

This easterly shove is visible as you drive up onto a stretch of rangeland just south of the Oldman River, crossing along Highway 22, but you have to be looking where you're going, not gazing at the sweeping span of the Livingstone Range to the west. Straight ahead, the line of mountains abruptly changes to a west-to-east track – what at first glance looks like a solid 10-kilometre wall of mountains from Syncline Mountain to Prairie Bluff. It's the first in a series of easterly jogs in the mountain front, courtesy of the Lewis Fault, that continue well into Montana. Again the critical connection between prairie grass and mountain pass reveals itself. (From Prairie Bluff to Waterton Lakes National Park the line of mountains returns to a northwest/southeast orientation before heading east once again toward Chief Mountain.)

The Lewis Thrust, however, did not leave the mountains the way we experience them today. That work was left for the glaciers. It took snow, ice and gravity to turn what were once gentle mountains and rolling plains into the Castle's peaks.

Rings of multi-coloured argillite on Drywood Mountain; lichen on Whistler Mountain.

## Melting Glaciers and Immerging Histories

*"Twenty thousand years ago the Rockies were an icebox."*

— Gary Ferguson

*"... glaciers take action and respond to their surroundings. They are sensitive to smells and they listen. They make moral judgments and they punish infractions"*

— Julie Cruikshank

Glaciers no longer grace the high alpine of the Castle. Gone are the frozen reservoirs of ancient pollen with their clues to atmospheric conditions that might tell us what life was like hundreds of thousands of years ago. Misplaced are the stories of snow and ice from histories deposited in the hairline cracks across limestone cliffs or buried beneath rich prairie soil. Instead we're left to crunch and cling to residual snow and ice from more recent cold snaps, piled at the base of glacial relics – narrow chimneys and steep headwalls – to remind us of what frozen time might have felt and sounded like. These cold bits and pieces, however, tell us little else of glaciations' ultimate consequences in the Castle.

To appreciate the force of ancient ice you have to look to the land's bigger scars – the long u-shaped South and West Castle valleys or the steep-walled canyons near the Front Range headwaters – and create your own stories. Sometimes it is hard to distinguish ice-scoured landscape from rain- and wind-sculpted rock. It is all a work in concert. Perhaps the series of steep and ragged cirques and their knife-edge arêtes along the Flathead Range give the hiker the most sweeping visual and visceral sense of past glacial movement in the Castle.

The earliest of the major ice ages is thought to have occurred around two million years ago. With each cold period temperatures plunged, locking wide swaths of the continent in an icy grip lasting thousands of years. No one is really sure how many times North America actually entered and left the freezer, but it is with some certainty that only two continental ice sheets reached into southwestern Alberta. This ancient ice never fully reached into the Castle, however. Glaciation in the mountains was to occur on a more elevated stage.

Unlike the massive continental ice sheets that covered the plains, Cordilleran glaciation remained loyal to the Rocky Mountains. Until its final retreat about 10,000 years ago, winter came to the Castle and mostly never left. Snow accumulated faster than it could melt, becoming deep, then deeper still. The snow turned into rivers of ice, then into larger glaciers. Eventually ice over a kilometre deep in places spread across the mountains as far south as Colorado. Instead of staying put, minor advances and retreats ground snow and ice into every nook and cranny, polishing the sides of mountains, scouring cliffs and sharpening knife-edge ridges.

As Cordilleran ice crossed the Continental Divide and entered the Castle the leading edge of the massive Laurentide Ice Sheet was advancing southwest from Hudson Bay across the continent. Exactly where and how these two ice giants met is still a matter of debate among geologists. More likely the rendezvous was a drawn-out affair between two wary rivals than a

Spionkop Ridge. Melting glaciers moved millions of years of rock out of the Front Range.

clash of titans. Geologists exploring the evidence have found material from the Canadian Shield up to elevations of 1580 metres along the Front Range valleys, indicating that Laurentide ice knocked on the Castle's door at its eastern edge. Along the northern edge, however, these erratics never reached the same heights. In a cool rebuke, fingers of alpine ice over 300 metres thick pushed out of the Gladstone, South Castle and West Castle valleys, stalling the advances of the continental ice just north and east of Beaver Mines.

The end of the glacial assault gave way to a new landscape. Meltwater flowed east and pooled against the retreating Laurentide ice, forming numerous, often expansive, glacially dammed lakes. Ice dams were prone to failure, resulting in frequent floods spilling along the icy margin. Rivers, now flush with glacial melt, began to carve up the land they had once helped build. This massive era of erosion and renovation is most noticeable in the Castle's Front Range canyons where Yarrow, Drywood and Pincher creeks wore away 70 million years of rock, leaving behind stoic cliff faces of hardier layers.

Freshly deposited soil on the flatlands and in the coulees invited a determined new growth of vegetation, which early on possibly resembled open tundra. That was before wetter and warmer weather brought more tropical vegetation. Grazing fauna, exotic in today's terms – mammoths, camels, large bison, helmeted musk-oxen and paleohorses, likely from the south – moved to inhabit the guiltless landscape. Bison did not appear on the southern Alberta plains until about 10,500 years ago. Following in the tracks of the grassland grazers, humans moved along the ice-free corridor.

As the ice disappeared across the plains, glaciers continued to grip the mountains. There is a common misconception, however, that today's northern Rocky Mountain glaciers are the remnants of the great Cordilleran ice field. The remaining alpine glaciers were actually formed during North America's Little Ice Age, sometimes referred to as the Cavell Glaciation, which began around 1200 CE. By the time this cold snap ended in the mid-1800s glaciers were all but gone from the Castle. South of the border, however, 150 of them continued to grace the alpine of the Crown of the Continent. Today some 37 small icefields still hang on in Glacier National Park. As the climate continues to change, the park will likely lose the last of its namesake ice formations long before the end of this century.

# A Land Inhabited

*"The streams of the northwest plains run cloudy with the powdery residue of the continental backbone."*

— John C. Jackson, *The Piikani Blackfeet: A Culture under Siege*

*It is a paradox that we climb alpine ridges to escape humanity only to arrive at the beginning, to the water and rock that bring life to the land below. One might think of hiking up into the Castle not as escape but as moving back in time against the flow of an impending civilization.*

— Journal entry, October 2005

Imagining a land void of humans is a lot easier and certainly less risky than describing a place inhabited by people – physical and natural processes being arguably more definitive and certainly less divisive than the fluidity and folly of human activity. But to understand developments in the Castle today we need to understand the history of regional settlement and land use, a history that for the most part took place in the prairies and the lower valleys. These were not mountain cultures, not in the traditions of Andean or Himalayan civilizations. Those that settled along the northern Rocky Mountain backbone were plains or valley people. They lived closer to the smell of grass and sage than of spruce and fir. The mountains were not necessarily home but they were essential. They offered sustenance and spirituality for many. In that sense the Castle was as much respected commons as contested or conquered grounds. Where has this indigenous narrative gone?

Popular versions like to present human history as they do natural history – a linear offering of facts and dates, a timeline of selected events and personalities. The more important or dramatic the occasion and the more colourful the characters, the more prominent is their position on the timeline and the more significant are the perceived historical consequences. This is not to say the roles of events and individuals are not critical to the understanding of our past, but who is deciding what or who is important and why? As Leslie Robertson states in her fascinating ethnography of Fernie, B.C., and the East Kootenays, "Popularized accounts of European settlement effectively erased the relationships between indigenous knowledge and the land." Historians were once in agreement that the mountains of the Crown of the Continent were rarely if ever used by people before the arrival of European explorers (Crown of the Continent, 7). Nothing could be further from the truth. Brings-Down-the-Sun was clear about this when he told Walter McClintock the story of the Old North Trail:

> "There is a well-known trail we call the Old North Trail. It runs north and south along the Rocky Mountains. No one knows how long it has been used by the Indians. My father told me it originated in the migration of a great tribe of Indians from the distant north to the south,

Heading north on Duck Lake Road from the Blackfeet Reservation in Montana toward Castle country. The thin profile of Chief Mountain juts skyward in the distance.

and all the tribes have, ever since, continued to follow in their tracks …
The Old North Trail is now becoming overgrown with moss and grass,
but it was worn so deeply, by many generations of travellers, that the
travois tracks and horse trail are still plainly visible …

In many places the white man's roads and towns have obliterated the
Old Trail. It forked where the city of Calgary now stands. The right fork
ran north into the Barren Lands as far as people live. The main trail ran
south along the eastern side of the Rockies, at a uniform distance from
the mountains, keeping clear of the forest and outside of the foothills …
My father once told me of an expedition from the Blackfeet that went
south by the Old Trail to visit the people with dark skins … They were
absent four years. It took them 12 moons of steady travelling to reach
the country of the dark-skinned people, and 18 moons to come north
again. They returned by a longer route through the "High Trees" or
Bitterroot country, where they could travel without danger of being seen.
They feared going along the North Trail because it was frequented by
their enemies …

I have followed the Old North Trail so often that I know every
mountain, stream and river far to the south as well as toward the
distant north."

— Brings-Down-the-Sun,
quoted by Walter McClintock in *The Old North Trail*

## Across Time and Territory

*Creator Sun lived all alone in the spiritual places for ages, no one*
*else to be with, and naturally he got lonely for some kind of life to be*
*with. One day he gathered the space dust and spit on it to make it*
*into clay. He had the future in mind … "I must make something in*
*my own way – something that will look like my image … "*
— Percy Bullchild, *The Sun Came Down: The History of the World as*
*My Blackfeet Elders Told It*

Whether by the Creator or by paleolithic circumstances, ancestors of the Plains Indians and all the First Nations peoples that came to live within the Crown of the Continent and on the edges of the Castle go back to the earliest North Americans. Archaeological evidence claims Neolithic bands of hunters migrated down the eastern flanks of the Rocky Mountains along an ice-free corridor that formed as the continental ice sheet pulled back. A line is drawn between archaeologists who believe the Paleoindians arrived no earlier than 14,000 years ago and a persistent minority who assert they reached North America at least 30,000 years ago (Krech 1999, 35). The mystery of who came first and when will not be solved anytime soon, if at all. So, like the hunter/gatherers at the centre of this dispute, it is maybe best to move on.

Human history on the prairies and in the mountain valleys is really a story of convergence – what historian Theodore Binnema calls "mixing and merging." For centuries after the push into the heart of the New World, small, diverse communities continued to move in and out of the northwestern plains, coming in contact with and pursuing herds of mammoth, mastodon and other ice-age herbivores. As the climate changed, so did the plants and animals. After an era which saw the mass extinction of the Continent's mega-fauna, bison ultimately became the dominant mammal grazing the grasslands. The climate became more steppe than tundra and civilization changed accordingly.

Eventually the climate stabilized and a more permanent human presence on the plains endured. Customs and technologies evolved. So did trade and commerce. Where vested interests and territories overlapped, clans formed coalitions. Larger groups were often fashioned to guard against hostile parties, share resources and keep tabs on the large, roaming herds of bison. These coalitions were dynamic and often contradictory. Enemies in one region might be allies in another, with terms of agreement constantly in negotiation. Bands were also linked by kinship, but these were not static either, as Theodore Binnema points out, because family ties often crossed ethnic lines.

This movement and alignment of peoples brought a vibrant civilization to the West, the evidence of which is usually overlooked in conventional historical accounts. As the last ice age ended, family, friends and foes extended over an area of grassland larger than Alberta and Saskatchewan combined, between the Mississippi River and the Rocky Mountains. As the ice finally melted out of the mountain passes and people were able to cross in both directions, the inhabitation of the continental northwest – at least 350 generations of men and women living in and transforming the landscape – was pretty much complete, even if the relationships continued to shift.

By the early 18th century the Crown of the Continent was shared territory for a diversity of peoples: Stoney, Siksika, Kainai, Piikani, Flathead, Shoshone and Ktunaxa. Within the commons of the Castle, Siksika, Piikani, Kainai and Ktunaxa were the predominant groups hunting, gathering tipi poles, collecting stone and seeking spiritual renewal.

**Blackfoot Nation**

> Nitawahsi is the name of our territory. Our ancient stories tell us that
> we were given this territory by Ihtsi-pai-tapi-yop our Creator and
> Essence of Life … Our traditional territory extended from Ponoka-si-
> sahta south to Otahkoi-tah-tayi. We lived along the eastern slopes of
> the Rocky Mountains and eastward beyond Omahski-spatsi-koyii …
> We knew every detail of this land. Our people travelled constantly
> through it and their trails are well marked …

> — Glenbow Museum:
> *Nitsitapiisinni: The Story of the Blackfoot People*

At the height of their dominance throughout the Northwest Plains, the Blackfoot controlled a large territory east of the Castle. Stretching from the Continental Divide, Blackfoot territory spanned more than half of present-day Alberta, most of Montana and western parts of Saskatchewan. Beyond this acknowledged territory the Blackfoot, in ever-shifting coalitions with the Sarcee, Sioux, Assiniboine Cree and Gros Ventre, were in command of the trade and resources of an even larger area during much of the 18th century. At the peak of their dominance in the latter years of that century the Blackfoot were successful in blocking most of the travel into the Castle and over the Continental Divide from both directions.

As coalitions broke down, skirmishes increased and the buffalo grew scarcer, local associations and subsistence within the Blackfoot nation shifted. Various groups began to establish stronger geographical ties with more distinct regions within Nitawahsi. The Siksika typically roamed the foothills and plains to the north and east, while the Kainai were more prominent in the middle territory. Meanwhile, the Piikani, the largest of the Niitsitapi nations, established themselves more to the south along the eastern edge of the Rocky Mountains and closest to the Castle. Deep in Blackfoot territory and protected by the mountains, the Piikani were in all probability the last of the Blackfoot to establish formal relationships with the European traders. Like all Plains peoples, the Piikani relied on their home territory to survive. They also fiercely defended against incursions, an active resistance that discouraged traders from travelling into Piikani territory.

Eventually, in order to deal directly with the Europeans and not broker trade through the Cree and Métis, the Piikani guided traders such as Peter Fidler into their territory. During his winter in their camps Fidler discovered that Piikani were particularly adept at acquiring beaver. Whether the Piikani obtained their supply directly from the surrounding wilderness or reluctantly traded for it with their Ktunaxa neighbours was of little consequence to Fidler and other traders. At the time, European gentlemen had a hankering for beaver felt hats and traders were anxious to get a steady supply regardless of the strained relations between Piikani and Ktunaxa. Shortly after Fidler's trip trading posts were built along the South Saskatchewan River, including the Hudson's Bay Company's Chesterfield House at the confluence of the Bow River with the Red Deer, to take advantage of this new relationship with the Piikani and other Blackfoot (Jackson 2000; Binnema).

When not travelling for trade, hunting, defending their territory or raiding others, the Blackfoot and in particular the Piikani oriented themselves away from the plains and more toward the mountains. As winter approached, groups would congregate in the sheltered valleys

Beaver skull along the Castle River. More than the hunt for bison, it was the trade in beaver with the Blackfoot and Ktunaxa that brought Europeans closer to the mountains and the Castle.

and coulees within the shadow of the Front Range. Areas like the Cut Bank Valley in northern Montana and along the Oldman River near the Piikani's present-day reserve were favoured wintering grounds. Extended hunting forays into the Castle provided them with additional food and firewood to subsist through the winters. Before long these would become winters of discontent, the start of a rapid decline that eventually led to treaty and reserves.

By the early 1800s the powerful Blackfoot Coalition was near collapse. The Cree had allied with the Métis and together they began to forcibly push the Niitsitapi frontier southward. Now in a territorial war, the once dominant Blackfoot Nation allowed the Tsuu T'ina (Sarcee) from the north and the Assiniboine Stoney to settle within the northern fringes of traditional Piikani territory along the Bow River. (The Cree and the Blackfoot made formal peace in 1871.)

The Blackfoot suffered a further setback with the stroke of a pen when the Lame Bull Treaty of 1855 effectively divided the Piikani Nation along the 49th parallel and designated the majority to the vast Blackfeet Reservation in northern Montana. After another smallpox epidemic ravaged the Blackfoot in the early 1860s, Northern Piikani ranks and territory were so depleted they could offer little resistance by the time of the first wave of European settlers came west under the Dominion Lands Act of 1872.

While the Blackfoot struggled in a diminishing territory the bison were rapidly dying. South of the border, railways had pushed into the plains, bringing more settlers and more guns. Bison already suffering under the charge of horses and heavy artillery were trapped. Cut down mercilessly by a fresh line of fire along the railway's advance, most of the remaining herds moved north. In an ironic and dreadful twist of fate the bison, their territory and numbers depleted to the point of no recovery,[3] were now at the mercy of a Blackfoot nation that also was depleted and starving. In 1882, a herd of bison found in the Sweet Grass Hills of northern Montana provided the Blackfoot with one last communal hunt. Four animals shot in the same area two years later proved to be the last known wild buffalo killed by the Blackfoot.

The international boundary that helped to define the Lame Bull Treaty, informally agreed upon in 1818 and established in 1848, remained invisible until surveyors from the Dominion and the United States began placing a line of cairns across the prairies in the spring of 1873 (LaDow, 86). Treaty Seven was only four years away. The Piikani had felt the impact of this arbitrary "line of civilization" (as it was often referred to by non-native leaders) – and the burdens of the past five decades – as harshly as any Plains nation. Once the largest nation in the Blackfoot Confederacy and the last holdout against the European incursion, the Piikani would be the smallest Blackfoot nation to take treaty in Canada.

---

3       Estimates vary, but by 1880 the number of bison was pegged as low as 100 in the U.S. and eight in Canada. – Dawn Walton, "Were bison one of globalization's first victims?" *The Globe and Mail*, July 31, 2007, A3.

## Ktunaxa Nation

*It runs through the middle of my
house. My home is on both sides.*
— Chief David of the Tobacco
Plains Band, Ktunaxa Nation,
when asked in 1887 about the
boundary between Canada
and the United States.
(quoted in Robertson, 25)

For thousands of years, Ktunaxa
territory (pronounced k-too-nah-ha)
comprised parts of northern Montana,
Washington, Idaho and southern
Alberta, including the Castle. The
rich mountain valleys in the heart of
the Rocky Mountains, especially west
of the Continental Divide, provided
the Ktunaxa with ample resources,
but long-standing traditions and
connections to the buffalo indicate
they were also once a prominent people
on the Plains. The Raven's Nest band
in particular, until they were virtually
wiped out by smallpox, lived east of
the Divide, in what today is called
Crowsnest Pass. After the devastating
smallpox epidemic that raced through
the northwest plains in 1781, and
faced with continuing attacks from
their eastern enemies, the Ktunaxa
never again resided east of the Divide
(Binnema, 81, 128).

## Modern Blackfoot

Today most Piikani, Siksika
and Kainai continue to live
close to their ancestral home.
While many have taken up cattle ranching, some traditional
Blackfoot land use remains.
Whether living on or off the
reserve, the Blackfoot continue to hunt game and gather
plants for food and medicines
on the fragments of their traditional territory made available to them through treaty.
Horses also remain impor-
tant in Blackfoot society. Specific to the Castle, both the
Piikani and the Kainai harvest
young lodgepole pine for tipi
construction and collect cer-
emonial paint and plants.

The population on the Piikani reserve is currently 2,200
people. About 60 per cent
of band members live in the
town of Brocket, while the
remainder are largely spread
out on the reserve's approximately 45,000 hectares of
prairie. The Kainai is the largest First Nation reserve in
area (136,264.6 hectares) in
Canada and has the second-
largest on-reserve population,
with 7,437 members (all fig-
ures 2005).

Isolated somewhat by the mountains, the Ktunaxa spoke a language unique among Native linguistic groups in North America. "Ktunaxa" actually translates as "licks the blood," referring to the strong dependence on hunting in their culture. After their retreat to the Flathead and Columbia River valleys the Ktunaxa still crossed the mountains to hunt bison on the plain, but since they were no longer in a position to track the herds year round, bison became less of a staple. Instead the Ktunaxa hunted deer, fished and trapped, and gathered plants such as bitterroot, camas, mosses, wild onions, huckleberries, saskatoons and chokecherries to supplement their diet.

View into the Flathead River Valley from North Kootenay Pass. The rich mountain valleys to the west of the Castle provided the Ktunaxa with ample resources early in their existence.

Although the Rocky Mountains were passable, they proved to be a barrier to the flow of trade and goodwill from east to west and vice versa. As late as the beginning of the 19th century, European goods were still few and far between in the Crown of the Continent west of the Divide. The Ktunaxa primarily traded with the Flathead, Shoshone and Crow further to the south. None of these peoples were as well equipped as those of the powerful Northern Coalition led by the Blackfoot, who had been trading with Europeans for decades. More than restricting exchange, the mountains blocked the bison, and with only minimal access to European goods, Ktunaxa hunting trips into the Plains were fraught with danger. A hunting trip would almost certainly need as much vigilance against raiding Blackfoot parties as it would for locating bison.

Ktunaxa territory, however, was considered rich in beaver, and both the Hudson's Bay Company and the North West Company were anxious to establish commercial alliances with the Ktunaxa. During his trip into Piikani territory in 1792 Peter Fidler also made contact with the Ktunaxa near the Oldman River Gap. In the early 1800s David Thompson of

**A'saani**

The Piikani found vitality in special ceremonies and daily rituals to seek success in hunting and warfare and guidance in personal and community health. In their ceremonies they often used a'saani, a sacred paint found in a specific site in the Castle the Piikani refer to as Crow Eagle. The ritual for finding paint would last for four days and four nights. Band members would gather, pray to the spirits and then begin their search for the paint. Prayers were considered answered when paint was found. A community celebration and feast concluded the ceremony. (Adapted from a brochure for Andy Russell-I'tai sah kòp Wildland Park.)

the North West Company pushed over the Divide north of Niitsitapi territory into the Rocky Mountain Trench and opened up direct trade links with the Ktunaxa.

To avoid crossing through the heart of Blackfoot territory the Ktunaxa were encouraged by the NWC to trade at the company's newly built post along the banks of the North Saskatchewan River, Rocky Mountain House. While this post was farther from the heart of Blackfoot territory than its HBC counterparts were, getting there was still an arduous journey from the Tobacco Plains. The Ktunaxa were under constant threat from the Blackfoot, who still controlled the eastern slopes of the Rockies. To the south the Ktunaxa travelled less and less through the Castle and consequently, after years of disuse, traditional trails over the mountains became "very much encumbered with wind fall wood ..." (Binnema, 168–184).

The difficult trail conditions over the Divide would impede but not prevent government-sanctioned explorers such as George Simpson, John Palliser, James Hector and Thomas Blakiston from crossing into Ktunaxa land in the years to come. The wind-blown trails would especially influence the route Blakiston would eventually take through the Castle in 1858. With each crossing into Ktunaxa territory these explorers, set on "securing possessions and rights of discovery," documented the landscape with their journals, maps and surveys while bringing back their own descriptions of Ktunaxa life and customs.

Blakiston's accounts are worth mentioning. According to Irene Spry, Blakiston " ... never failed to receive manifestations of goodwill" from the Ktunaxa, whom he described as "honest," "civil and "hospitable." First and foremost, Blakiston was a soldier and secondly a scientist committed to the British monarchy and its colonial subjects. He was eager to press upon all he met the duty of his mission:

> I made a rule never to hide from Indians ... and to go to them as soon as I knew their proximity ... I told them plainly for what reason we had been sent to the country: that Her Majesty was always glad to hear of their welfare, and that any message which they might have for Her I would take down in writing.

The Ktunaxa, possibly impressed by this veiled offer of support, confided in Blakiston the ill treatment they were receiving at the hands of traders and the Blackfoot and the depletion of wild animals they were witnessing. By extending their trust, the Ktunaxa seemed ready to welcome the foreigners.

Today the Ktunaxa Nation, compromising of seven bands – Columbia Lake, Lower Kootenay, St. Mary's, Shuswap, Tobacco Plains, Confederated Salish and Kootenay – covers approximately 70,000 square kilometres (27,000 square miles) within their traditional territory on both sides of the international border. The major trails they used to cross the Continental Divide still carry the names North, Middle and South Kootenay Pass, where "Kootenay" or "Kootenai" is a colonial derivative of "Ktunaxa."

## Blackfoot/Ktunaxa Relations

Partially separated by the permeable wall of mountains, Ktunaxa and Blackfoot ancestors lived in relative accord for thousands of years. This was still a time when the Castle could be considered, for the most part, common ground. Important routes west over the Continental Divide became established

### Camas

Both Blackfoot and Ktunaxa gathered camas from the moister meadows in the Castle. Whether on purpose or by accident camas also became a staple up and down the Old North Trail. When cooked the root was a main sweetener before the introduction of sugar. The root was dug while the plant was in bloom, from mid-June to mid-July, then cooked, sun-dried and stored in sacks for winter use. Often it was pounded along with saskatoons into cakes. As well, the camas bulbs were roasted in large, covered pits. After the pit was opened to retrieve the bulbs, children would gather to suck the sweet syrup that had collected on the twigs and grass. The fresh-roasted camas bulb has the texture of a chestnut and tastes like molasses (Grinnell, 204).

"roads to the buffalo" as John C. Jackson put it, and encouraged cross-cultural trade. But the introduction of horses and firearms, the outbreaks of smallpox, and the expansion of European trade quickly changed these peoples' relationships to the land and to each other.

The Ktunaxa were the first to get horses. Both Flathead Rendezvous within the Crown of the Continent and Shoshone Rendezvous further to the south were well-established indigenous trading hubs. The trade route followed the west side of the Continental Divide from Zuñi and Pecos territory, and goods were moving frequently north and south by the time the Spanish introduced horses into Mexico in the late 1500s. By 1720 horses had made their way north to Ktunaxa territory. Horses on the Plains took a more circuitous trade route, travelling from the southwest deserts into Middle Missouri and the Eastern Plains. These were the territories of the Hidatsa, Mandan, Assiniboine Cree and Gros Ventre – all trading partners within the powerful Northern Coalition led by the Blackfoot. According to Theodore Binnema, horses were grazing the short grass of Niitsitapi territory by 1740.

The introduction of firearms did not have the same bilateral history, and consequently their trajectory onto the plains skewed the balance of power. For the most part, guns came one way – west, with the European fur traders – arriving here in the mid-1700s. Although the Ktunaxa were first to get the horse, the Blackfoot were first to get the rifle, and thus were the Ktunaxa vulnerable whenever they were in Blackfoot territory.

Despite tensions, temporary alliances were still made in order to take advantage of European trade, which was becoming increasingly influential. The Ktunaxa wanted access to buffalo and European goods. The Blackfoot regarded the buffalo as their own, but when animals were plentiful, they would tolerate Ktunaxa hunting parties. The Piikani, because of their proximity to the mountain passes, would offer access to hunting grounds in exchange for beaver pelts as well as horses. But according to Theodore Binnema, anything more than a temporary arrangement between Piikani and Ktunaxa was impossible. Kainai and Siksika were known to raid Ktunaxa for horses, and retaliation mounted by the Ktunaxa usually targeted the Piikani because of their closeness to Ktunaxa land.

The relationship between Ktunaxa and Blackfoot was further upset when the North West Company pushed over the mountains north of Blackfoot territory to open up direct links with the Ktunaxa, and also later when trade with the upstart Pacific Fur Company began moving goods along the Columbia River system far from Blackfoot influence. No longer profitable intermediaries in the European trade market, the Niitsitapi felt growing hostility toward the Ktunaxa. The commons of the Castle entered a new era. It was now a place of conflict, a ground on which to wrest territorial control for trade and bison. The Blackfoot kept close watch over the mountain passes, until European explorers came with their own agenda of territorial conquest.

## Putting the Castle on the Modern Map: The Traders and Explorers

*Travelling through southwestern Alberta or northern Montana into the Castle is an opportunity to go beyond the boundaries of popular history, to revisit and revise the story of European settlement in the Crown of the Continent.*

— Journal entry, September 2005

John Palliser sat on his horse and looked away to the north over the prairies. How far beyond the curve of the horizon did the rolling prairies stretch on? What kind of country lay there? Rich grasslands? Dry sandy sagebrush? Or sculpted badlands? Where did the forests of the North begin? And where did the plains meet the shining mountains to the northwest? Was there any way through those mountains to the Pacific Ocean? And where did the boundary between United States and British Territory run? He could not stay to find out. He had to go back to his home in Ireland after a long hunting trip in the prairies and the mountains of the Upper Missouri.[4]

— Irene Spry in *The Palliser Expedition*

---

4        Ten years later, Palliser did return to the prairies and mountains of southern Alberta, as leader of the British North American Exploring Expedition.

The noble explorer alone on horseback atop some rock outcrop, shading his eyes as he peers westward before venturing forth into the vast unknown is a popular image. It continues to dominate the historical and day-to-day perspectives in the Crown of the Continent. But it is an outdated point of view. It inevitably leads us to imagine that first contact was only made when European explorers pushed west into Native American territory. It also unfortunately validates what Gary Paul Nabhan calls the "heroic act of discovery" which establishes a territory as if it did not previously exist, at the expense of the more tangled "art of discovering" that assures us of how little we actually understand about the past and how much there is still to learn about the ground on which we stand.

To accept the story of "heroic discovery" would be to believe that the Blackfoot and the Ktunaxa were passively unaware of the world beyond their traditional hunting grounds. Instead, time and time again indigenous hunting and trading parties travelled far beyond their camps, past the camps of their

Statue of two warriors astride their horses: one of four sculptures by Blackfeet artist Jay Laber at each entrance to the Blackfeet Reservation.

neighbours and those of their neighbours' neighbours. Before European settlers ever set foot on prairie soil both Blackfoot and Ktunaxa had already ventured far to the south, into Spanish settlements. On these excursions they learned the extent of the country and the customs of other indigenous groups, as John Ewers's study of the Blackfeet pointed out. Travelling their own well-worn trails, therefore, the Blackfoot and the Ktunaxa were the ones establishing contact with the Europeans, brokering trade and leading explorers through the Crown of the Continent and into the Castle.

The first notable European/indigenous relationships would have been established through trade. As early as the late 1700s traders were travelling close to and possibly through the Castle. Little is known of these excursions, if indeed they occurred. Much of the communication was by word of mouth and not recorded. What journals and maps did exist were sequestered by company superiors worried about competition and settlement. The traders were there to safely establish partnerships with indigenous trappers and maximize the furs heading to Europe, not to secure lands for the Dominion. Settlement would just bring unwanted competition for resources and upset a balance of trade already established. To ensure goodwill and economic security, the Hudson's Bay Company encouraged its employees and officers to form connections with influential families and even approved marriage (Robertson, 9).

Most accounts now assert that indigenous peoples were "active and sophisticated" participants in the productive northwest plains trade economy. The arrival of European-influenced trade did not immediately lead to economic dependence on European wares or to cultural and social decline. The Blackfoot and the Ktunaxa maintained their own world view. Accordingly, the Blackfoot initially integrated Europeans into their way of life as Napikwan (Oldman Persons) (Binnema, 114–115).

Lucrative trade also brought greed and a disregard for established protocol. Independent trappers looking to capitalize on existing markets would often venture into controlled territories. Many went farther still, looking for new resources in uncharted lands. Without proper consent from the indigenous trappers or traders these often romanticized mountain men took huge risks and probably did more harm than good with regard to existing partnerships. Sometimes they would make quick alliances but these would be poorly communicated or not recognized by indigenous trappers. As a result the independent trapper was often seen as an interloper and thief and he often paid for his cavalier act with his life. Most accounts of the daring trapper were largely fictionalized reports from the pens of creative historians.

Back east and over in Europe the early-19th-century mindset, fuelled by epic tales of frontier adventure, was still fixated on a vast and mythical Great North American Desert. From its colonies around the globe, a steady stream of exotic products and exploration stories inundated Britain. Magic lantern slide shows and lectures on world geography became popular forms of entertainment (Robertson, 8). Charles Darwin's trip on the *Beagle* was still a decade away, but even so, a new age of scientific discovery and literacy was emerging. Any sense of indigenous connection and settlement was certainly different from what the majority was prepared to understand.

Even with Aaron Arrowsmith's revised map of the North American interior and the journals of Lewis and Clark in hand, the West remained a mythical landscape. As explorers-in-waiting looked out from the eastern margins they perceived an empty land. Upon entering they found no permanent settlements, no clues of occupancy that they could understand. What the explorers lacked in intimacy they made up with assumptions, leaving those writing about North American wilderness to their own romantic notions. More contemporary writers with the benefit of hindsight, such as Irene Spry in her detailed account of the Palliser expedition, also tended to drift toward the notion of a savage wilderness rather than any pre-existing civilization:

> The Prairies of British North America were still then a wild, sparsely peopled waste. From the single tiny settlement at Red River where Winnipeg now stands, they stretched westward into dim, unimagined distances ...

> — *The Palliser Expedition: The Dramatic Story of Western Exploration 1857–1860*

The omission of indigenous people from the land, however, was more than a naive lack of understanding or literary device. It also helped open the way for settlement. International law at the time recognized sovereignty on three criteria: cession, conquest and occupation of territory (Robertson, 10). In the tradition of imperial adventure, British governments and trading companies sent expeditions to document and map the empty prairies and the trackless passes through the mountains. If no other civil nation or state had entered a region, the land was deemed empty. Anyone found on the land but not connected to a *recognized* nation or state would have no civil presence or possession. On such terms the West was ripe for dominion – finders keepers.

Remarks made at the time by Sir George Simpson of the HBC, concerning Lewis and Clark's recently completed expedition up the Missouri River, offer insight into the need for explorers to uphold the deep, dark secret of an empty land ...

> In order to give the exploration as much as possible the air of a Voyage of Discovery, and to make it appear as if they were exploring and taking possession of an unknown land (though in fact the Country of the Interior was well known to traders from Canada) the Americans as they went along bestowed new names on rivers, mountains, etc.... forgetting or affecting to forget ... previous surveyed routes and possessed territories.
>
> (Simpson 1822 quoted in Rich 1947 at 183, from Robertson, 9)

Of course, Simpson's rant against Lewis and Clark was as much an admission of his own competitive pride and sense of duty. The international boundary in the West was still up for grabs and clarification of territorial possession required formal documentation. "Title to territories included justifications on the grounds of first discovery, priority ... continued occupation and actual possession." wrote John Pelly, Governor of the HBC. In 1824 Pelly sent Simpson west to gather more accurate information from the Rocky Mountains.

Despite all the lust for new discoveries back home and commotion in the more settled territories to the north, south and east, it took another two decades after Simpson's expedition before any official government exploring party – American or British – ventured back into the heart of Blackfoot territory. While the bison still roamed the plains, the Ktunaxa, Piikani and Kainai still travelled freely throughout the Crown of the Continent. Rumblings from south of the 49th parallel, however, were forcing a shift in territorial control that would eventually impact First Nations and the Castle region.

### The Palliser Expedition

As the mid-1800s drew near, the u.s. government was financing expeditions to look for potential railway routes through the mountains to the Pacific Ocean. Some of these parties were known to be crossing into British territory on both sides of the mountains. The Hudson's Bay Company, still in control of the fur trade north of the 49th parallel, was becoming increasingly alarmed that the Piikani were dealing more and more with the American Fur Company to the south.

The hbc also recognized the importance of connecting the Great Plains with the Pacific. Surveyors like Peter Fidler and his North West Company rival David Thompson had made earlier trips over the mountains, but their records, in light of the more recent and aggressive u.s. approach to territorial control, were too focused on establishing trading routes and partnerships and not on claiming territory. The accuracy of Simpson's records was also questionable. They were certainly not precise enough to gauge a potential railway through the Rockies let alone determine the dividing line between two nations. Besides, it was common knowledge amongst the Ktunaxa, the Blackfoot and others that a more southerly route through the mountains than Simpson's existed.

In 1841 James Sinclair, with the aid of fellow Métis guides, had successfully led a group of emigrants across the prairies and over the Continental Divide to the lower Columbia River. Not satisfied with this route, in 1854 he led a second wagon train that included a sizeable herd of cattle over yet another mountain pass. It was a route he had talked about with explorer John Palliser six years earlier. But before Palliser could confirm the pass with his contemporary, Sinclair was killed during an attack on a u.s. outpost in the Columbia Valley. Palliser was able to talk to some of the settlers once they returned to Manitoba, however. It had taken "seven men, three women and several children" nine days to get through the mountains. They told Palliser they had crossed via the North Kootenay Pass. Could this be the sought-after southerly route?

While the Hudson's Bay Company concerned itself in large measure with expanding trade and routes over the mountains, the British government was getting anxious about borders and future settlement. They were interested in determining the West's potential for other forms of commerce: farming, mining, lumber milling. All these industries required information that could be translated into usable terms and procedures by the ruling class back in Britain and to be made relevant for the recruitment of a new and able pioneer. It was time to "discover" the new West.

Underwritten by the Treasury on behalf of the British Colonial Office and the Royal Geographic Society, Palliser set off in 1857 with scientists James Hector, Eugene Bourgeau and John Sullivan to explore the prairies and mountains. It was not simply a journey to find a suitable southern route through the Rockies, though that was Palliser's main personal objective, but a two-year expedition to gather scientific information on climate, soil, plants and animals, even astronomy. Scientists across Europe were eager for the British government to establish observatories throughout its "extensive dominion in all parts of the globe" (Spry, 87). Added to the expedition was the task of recording the earth's magnetic fields – not something one would consider a worthy expenditure en route to territorial expansion. In a time of increasing scientific theory and imperial destiny, however, every bit of empirical data was considered vital to the understanding of a region and to the success of the mission.

## Two Castles make a Windsor

Around the same time, Blakiston's expedition colleague James Hector also named a prominent mountain the "Castle." Hector's Castle Mountain rises from the Bow Valley west of Banff and is well known because of its visibility along the Trans-Canada Highway. In 1915, Blakiston's Castle was renamed Windsor Mountain because it resembled Windsor Castle in England. Castle and North Castle remain the names of Windsor's two most prominent peaks.

## North Kootenay Pass: Blakiston Enters the Castle

Pulled by the scientific hubris of the day, Palliser's expedition team was still short one magnetic observer. Thomas Blakiston, more soldier than scientist, was recruited and after three months learning how to use the complicated instruments he joined the main party. Early into the expedition he crossed swords with various members of the party, upset that he had to answer to non-military and younger personnel. Within the year Blakiston "threw off [Palliser's] command," left the main expedition and struck out on his own (Spry, 87).

Remaining loyal to the Royal Geographic Society, Blakiston continued to seek a southerly pass, map the territory and take magnetic readings. On the way south from Old Bow Fort (50 km west of present-day Calgary) his party found what were considered odds and ends of James Sinclair's trip through Kananaskis Pass before crossing the Highwood River. Next they crossed the Oldman River, which Blakiston initially referred to as the Belly. He also spotted a large dome-shaped mountain through a gap and named it after the famed naturalist John Gould. (Today gap and mountain are known respectively as Livingstone Gap and Tornado Mountain, Gould's Dome being reserved for a smaller mountain situated to the southeast.)

Blakiston was now on a roll. Staying along the eastern slopes he followed the base of a continuous ridge of mountains which he named the Livingstone Range after the great British explorer of Africa. Before turning west up what appeared to be the way through the mountains he took note of two other distinct mountains. One he named Castle Mountain; the other, farther to the southeast, he recognized as Chief Mountain, which he knew about from earlier reports by Palliser.

Windsor Mountain (formerly Castle Mountain), with the distinct Castle Peak, reveals itself from numerous vantage points. Here we see it from Drywood Mountain on the eastern edge of the Castle.

Entering the corridor leading to the Crowsnest Pass, Blakiston was told "many days of poor travel" lay ahead. Throughout his journey Blakiston had found fallen timber to be his greatest impediment. Listening to his guides he pushed further south, up the Castle River, where he connected with a trail heading up alongside the Carbondale. On August 21, 1858, Blakiston's party crossed over North Kootenay Pass and into the Flathead Valley. By taking the Carbondale River trail over the Continental Divide, Blakiston missed what would turn out to be the lowest-elevation and most accessible route through the southern Canadian Rocky Mountains: today's Crowsnest Pass.

"We are now on the watershed of the mountains, the great axis of America … a few steps farther and l gave a loud shout as I caught the first glimpse in a deep valley, as it were at my feet, of a feeder of the Pacifc Ocean. It was the Flathead River, a tributary of the Columbia. At the same moment the shots of my men's guns echoing among the rocks announced the passage of the first white man over the Kootanie Pass."

— Thomas Blakiston (Spry, 174)

Plaque commemorating Palliser's crossing over North Kootenay Pass in 1858.

Blakiston continued to explore the Flathead and Kootenay valleys west of the Castle for another ten days, even crossing over into u.s. territory at one point. Believing he had accomplished all he had been asked to do, he was guided back up the Flathead River, up the uncharted Kishinena Creek and over what is now known as South Kootenay Pass. He then followed down a drainage (now called Blakiston Creek) past what is now known as Blakiston Mountain to a series of lakes, which he named after another British naturalist, Charles Waterton. (The more southerly Akamina Pass would remain undiscovered by European explorers for another three years.)

Upon his return to Fort Edmonton Blakiston refused to hand over his report and maps to Palliser. Instead he sent them directly to the Royal Geographic Society. With this final act of obstinacy Blakiston sealed his fate regarding any more exploratory work in the Dominion and he returned to England.

Blakiston's experiences along with those of the other Palliser expeditions did more than confirm the presence of arable land (despite Palliser's own concerns about its aridity), lumber and minerals. Now on its own terms, the Dominion had documented a region no longer regarded as empty. Discoveries had been made and flags planted. Their reports marked a turning point in European perception of the West, in particular what would become southern Alberta, and opened the way for new developments. Stories of indigenous encounters like Blakiston's with the Ktunaxa, mixed with detailed descriptions of the region's natural history, gave the illusion of a clear understanding of the land and acceptance by First Nations peoples of colonial possession. European settlement and the eventual removal of the Piikani, Siksika, Kainai and Ktunaxa from the land were just around the corner.

### Treaty Seven and Removal from the Land

*In 1872 the Dominion Lands Act under John A. MacDonald's Conservative government provided 160 acres of land for a ten dollar registration fee to each head of a family. After cultivating 30*

*acres, showing the receipts for his crop and building a permanent*
*dwelling within three years he would receive title to the land.*
*An extensive advertising campaign throughout Western Europe*
*followed, to bring a wave of immigrants to the "Last, Best West."*

— Barry Potyondi, *Where the Rivers Meet:*
*A History of the Upper Oldman River Basin to 1939*

*"This is what I have seen in my dreams, this is the country for me."*

— Kootenai Brown

It is hard to disagree with Brown's revelation. The sweep of prairie into the Castle's mountains *is* dreamlike. One can well imagine what settlers arriving, lease in hand, saw from the numerous vantage points leading into this corner of "paradise." It was certainly nothing they had witnessed before: an unhindered mountain panorama from Prairie Bluff to Chief Mountain; wave after wave of hardy native grass; valleys crowded with cottonwood and wolf willow; and rivers flowing with clean mountain water. But whatever they saw, "Last, Best West" or not, it was still only a dream. No board had yet been nailed nor any seed planted; not a tree yet felled nor any grave dug.

The Canadian government, realizing dreams alone couldn't build a democratic union, felt the time for intensive settlement was at hand. A handful of Mounties could not expect to hold sway; the West had to be populated by loyal citizens. Key to the federal government's broad settlement plan was the confederation of resource-rich British Columbia into Canada. But before they would cede their colony, British Columbian politicians and developers demanded a railway to connect them to the rest of Canada. Inspired by the completion of the Union Pacific's transcontinental railway south of the border, Ottawa agreed to the demand and in 1871 British Columbia signed on to Confederation. Construction on the railway commenced immediately ("A Brief History of the Canadian Pacific Railway" at cprheritage.com).

A national railway dovetailed nicely with Ottawa's new National Policy: settle the West through immigration of productive farmers, export grain east and import goods west. The promise of private land ownership would be the necessary perk to spread this economic prosperity. The empire now had its westernmost province and the foundation for a real-estate- and agriculture-based economy. Others would follow to log trees, dig mines, drill oil to add resource extraction to the economic landscape. The land would rapidly become hemmed in by the federal government's new political-economic agenda.

Events south of the border and on the plains, however, were disrupting the plan to bring about European settlement. First Nations below the 49th parallel were refusing to be marshalled onto reservations and the u.s. Army was dispatched to force them. After the watershed Battle of the Little Big Horn in 1876 many Sioux escaped to Canada. Like the Sioux, the Nez Perce were also on the run north (LaDow, 43–45). Disputes over territory continued. The bison were disappearing. Starvation and disease were at hand. If it was the last West, it certainly wasn't the best one. Apprehensive of the situation and committed to

their promise of land to the new settlers – land they did not actually have the right to – the Canadian government took a hundred-year-old document and acted quickly.

In the Royal Proclamation of 1763 Britain had asserted jurisdiction over an extensive territory beyond their eastern colonies. In theory the Proclamation recognized that First Nations occupied Rupert's Land and that

The sweep of prairie into the Castle's mountains is dreamlike: Spionkop to Prairie Bluff along the Front Range and from Prairie Bluff to Table Mountain looking south from vantage point above the Gladstone Valley.

if the British Crown wished to acquire those rights, title must be purchased or transferred. The Proclamation also recognized aboriginal entitlement to the land's resources, stating that the Crown was merely establishing foreign rights under existing aboriginal authority. Now the federal government wanted the First Nations to cede their title so that lands and resources could be legally passed into either private ownership or federal rule.

On September 17, 1877, representatives from the Tsuu T'ina, Stoney, Siksika, Kainai and North Piikani peoples gathered at Blackfoot Crossing along the banks of the Bow River east of present-day Calgary to review and discuss treaty with government officials. The Blackfoot, hard-pressed by starvation, were being asked to give up land title in return for help adjusting to a new way of life. Fifty thousand square miles and "a direct relationship with the Crown" were on the table (Jackson 2000, 180). To the Blackfoot, land ownership was an abstraction. Even though trade had introduced the concept of private property, the importance of land had been primarily about negotiating territorial access to buffalo, not about sovereign rights. The land and animals as they knew them would still be there tomorrow and the day after that and on into the next hunting season. Why not then trade an abstraction like "land title" for immediate, tangible aid?

Five days after the gathering at Blackfoot Crossing commenced, Treaty Seven was signed. Reserves were quickly allocated. The Siksika were placed on 470 square miles close to the site of the treaty ceremonies. The Tsuu T'ina and Stoney settled farther west along the Bow River, in the foothills. The Kainai ended up with the largest reserve, 541 square miles of rolling prairie between the Belly and St. Mary rivers. The Piikani were installed along the benches and grasslands above the Oldman River in clear view of the Rocky Mountains.[5]

The size and location of these reserves and the stipends handed out were less than arbitrary. Each person accounted for was reserved the equivalent of two-tenths of a square mile. Each was given twelve dollars the first year and five dollars annually from then on. (Chiefs received twenty-

---

5        Across the Divide the Ktunaxa Nation have yet to relinquish title to their traditional lands. In 1993 the Ktunaxa Kinbasket Treaty Council began negotiating with the Canadian and British Columbia governments on their land claim.

five dollars annually, minor chiefs and councillors fifteen.) Ammunition would be provided for hunting on what was now government land, and supplies to begin farming and ranching were to be handed out as needed. For the Blackfoot, a way of life – hunting, gathering and trading – had come to an end.

Through the treaty process government officials got what they wanted and on the cheap. Less than two decades after Blakiston ventured into the Castle, the Blackfoot were moved off the land, paving the way for settlement and development.

## Limitless Land or Last Best West?

*What does it mean for one's home to disappear in less than a generation only to be reclaimed by another one's dream?*

— Journal entry, December 2006

Carving up a perceived wilderness for the sake of the Dominion may have been one thing but selling the Wild West to settlers was quite another, and easier said than done. "Winters are pleasant and healthful … conditions to make prosperity are there …" and "where a little capital and a little modicum of hard work guaranteed a family all it could wish for," trumpeted the promotional brochures for the Canadian Pacific Railway. But the brassy music fell on largely unresponsive ears. More than 25 years of government boosterism was slow to bring official settlement west, and by the turn of the 20th century only one-fifth of Canada's eventual total homestead entries had been recorded (LaDow, 84).

Some of the earliest homesteaders in southern Alberta immediately after Treaty Seven were Métis. Instead of benefiting from official settlement, however, many came west to escape aggressive European settlement and oppressive prejudices back east. Having been actively involved in the fur-trade economy, the Métis were well suited for life in the shadow of the Rockies, taking jobs as interpreters, guides and labourers or becoming early subsistence farmers, ranchers or sawmill operators (Potyondi, 31).

71

Abandoned homestead, with Windsor, Gladstone and Table Mountain in the distance.

Regardless whether escaping from or encouraged by the Dominion Lands Act, many settlers began to experience the harsh realities of the West. "Rain does not follow the plow" was becoming a well-worn maxim throughout the prairies. The dry conditions Palliser witnessed two decades before were turning out to be the norm. Without water or an adequate growing season, cultivating a quarter section proved to be a backbreaking proposition and many failed without ever harvesting a crop.

Up against the eastern slopes of the Rockies, where water was more plentiful but frost came early, the land turned out to be better suited for ranching than farming. Livestock – particularly cattle – and ranching values transferred well to the new West with its abundant fescue grasses and laissez-faire promise of open range and minimal government regulations. By the mid-1880s, with the bison gone, cattle grazing became the primary land use from Calgary to the u.s. border and beyond.

Most of the early ranchers in southern Alberta were from wealthy British backgrounds and as a result livestock came to represent wealth and power here as it did in England. To have land or access to land was one thing, but to put that land into production by grazing livestock on it was another matter entirely. Even those not of the established aristocracy could potentially enter the cattle business. Keeping tabs on the animals, rounding them up and bringing the herd to the free-market auction was pretty well the extent of operations and the economic payoff early on.

Contrary to the government's claims of democratic union through small freehold settlement, early development in the new West depended on concentrated wealth and large land holdings. The new national railway brought an expanding beef market to the rancher's front door, and the cattle industry grew dramatically. Jumping on the cash cow, cattlemen began competing for grazing leases on Crown land offered under the Dominion Lands Act. In 1885 just four cattle companies – the Cochrane, Bar U, Oxley and Walrond [later Waldron] ranches – controlled almost half of the leased land along the Eastern Slopes of the Rockies in southern Alberta ("Ranching History" in the *Canadian Encyclopedia* online).

The town of Pincher Creek, seen here from near the present-day Kootenai Brown Pioneer Museum, was incorporated in 1906. Windsor Mountain with its distinct looms in the background flanked by Prairie Bluff (Corner Mountain) on the left and Mount Gladstone on the right. Photo by Bert Riggall, courtesy of the Kootenai Brown Pioneer Village and Pincher Creek Historical Society.

The arrival of the railway, however, also brought a renewed interest in settlement along the Eastern Slopes. "Farmers were coming at an astonishing rate" into the Oldman River district, according to land agent A.E. Cox, quoted in Potyondi. With the government feeling the pressure of their own immigration policies, the large-scale ranchers received notice in 1892 that their leases were being cancelled to open the land up to the homesteaders. Steadily settlement took hold and a grid of barbed wire began to replace the open range. In 1899 alone, 300 new immigrants registered at the Pincher Creek land office. The NWMP's annual report for 1902 affirmed this wave of settlement: " ... to the north from Macleod to Nanton, to the east to Kipp, to the south to the boundary and west to Crow's Nest, nearly every available section of land has been either taken up or purchased" (Potyondi, 104).

Despite the influx of sodbusters and the decline of the large ranch, cattle production was still the major contributor to Alberta's fledgling economy and the strongest influence on the government's land-use policies. To further reinforce their economic and political power, ranchers turned to cooperation. In 1886 the Canadian Northwest Stock Association, later

## Crowsnest Pass

The Crowsnest Pass began as a string of settlements that reflected the distribution of coal mining properties in the late 19th and early 20th centuries. West of the divide the Crow's Nest Pass Coal Co. controlled the vast bulk of the coal in one major land holding. In Alberta huge blocks of property were not made available. Instead land was parcelled into 160-acre plots, forcing mining companies to lease or buy property by the quarter section. As a result, smaller mining companies worked individual properties, with towns springing up around the mines.

In the summer of 1978, a plebiscite was held to eliminate the duplication of services and expenditures. Almost 70 per cent of the 6,000 inhabitants voted to amalgamate Bellevue, Hillcrest, Frank, Blairmore and Coleman along with Improvement District No. 5 into a single municipality. The Municipality of Crowsnest Pass was officially incorporated on January 1, 1979. The municipality was enlarged 27 years later to include the northern portion of Improvement District No. 6, and it now borders on the Castle.

known as the Western Stock Growers' Association, came to represent most of the ranchers along the Eastern Slopes. The Association lobbied government on many fronts: better protection against rustlers; stronger quarantine for u.s. cattle; exclusion of sheep from the range; bounties on wolves; restrictions on squatters' rights. If any one issue united ranchers, however, it was control over range land, and in particular, water for their stock (Potyondi, 87–89).

After years of drought, ranchers and farmers were all well aware of the saying "if you didn't have water you were out of luck." Knowing that access to water could well save their operations as their dominance on the open range diminished, a strong cattle lobby convinced the government to give them control of major springs, rivers and creek headwaters as stock-watering reserves on Crown land. To access water upstream, ranchers often ceded lease land to homesteaders. In one illustration of such land dealings, Fred Godsal, a founding member of the Western Stock Growers' Association, ended up swapping nine-tenths of his 40,000-acre lease along the Castle River west of Pincher Creek in return for water access farther up in the Castle headwaters (Pincher Creek Historical Society, 47).

Looking out over the Shell Waterton gas plant with Drywood and Victoria Mountain in the background. Photo: Janet Main, 200. Ranchers have become an important voice in the movement to protect water sources and open landscape from industrial development along the Eastern Slopes of the Rocky Mountains.

It is interesting to note that the rancher lobby, once considered a major voice of power politics, privilege and self-interest in Alberta, has become a critical foundation in the movement to protect water sources and the concept of open landscape from industrial and recreational development – in particular, oil and gas, mining, logging and theme parks. Rancher-driven landowner groups and land trusts are doing what was once unheard of: teaming up with small rural landowners – the modern homesteader – to speak out against major developments on leased Crown land in southern Alberta.

No matter their rivalry, neither the rancher nor the homesteader was having an easy time of it, especially in the formative years of settlement. Quality land and optimum conditions were not always waiting at the end of a long journey from the homeland. The Dominion Lands Act, at least in theory, guaranteed possession of "rich fertile land" without a lot of red tape. The reality for the settler was different. While there was plenty of land available, much of the quality holdings were already reserved by the government for the railways and other major land developers. Those who came early found good, fertile

## Cows in the Castle

For four years I worked on and off as a ranch hand on the eastern and northern edges of the Castle. The fact that a greenhorn from the city with a limited knowledge of cows would be hired as a ranch hand speaks much for the generosity and openness of my employers. My time on the MX, Freeman, Stillridge and Kaotorati ranches, moving cows, birthing calves, fixing fence and listening to stories at the end of a day's labour, was instrumental in shaping my connection to this place – to the land and to those who live closest to the Castle's wild spaces.

When the federal government transferred control of the Eastern Slopes forest reserves to the province in the 1930s there were 3,778 grazing leases in Alberta covering over three million acres. Stocking rates eventually peaked in the 1950s and since then the number of cows on public land has been reduced significantly. Today only one-third as many cattle graze in the Castle as were allowed in the past.

Even with reduced herd numbers, the Castle remains an integral part of Alberta's Eastern Slopes ranching frontier. Its sheltered valleys, higher than average rainfall, and warm chinook winds which keep the hills bare of snow, continue to make it one of North America's preferred cattle-raising regions. Today cooperatives representing local ranches use the Castle for grazing. Each grazing cooperative hires a range rider, whose job it is to move cattle throughout the lease area and prevent overgrazing and streambank erosion – not always an easy task. Under provincial guidelines each ranch is allowed to move a set number of cows and their calves into the Castle from early June until early October when they are rounded up and moved back to the home ranch.

land with water. Those who came later with the boom often had to accept less than ideal conditions farther from town or purchase land from either the railway or the Hudson's Bay Company at a premium. With each wave of homesteaders trying to make a go of it, settlement moved toward the mountains and closer to the edge of the Castle.

Cows grazing along a seismic line near the Carbondale River.

# A Landscape Divided

*Humanity's increasing power to alter nature coincides with an unprecedented obliviousness of natural processes ... Where different modes of living collide, differences between forms of knowledge and belief with regard to nature can matter greatly.*

— Stephen Most,
*River of Renewal: Myth and History in the Klamath Basin*

As land privatization pushed toward the mountains, the Canadian government, like its counterpart south of the border, began setting aside parcels of public lands to protect the watersheds that supplied the communities and dryland farms downstream. Under a revised Dominion Lands Act in 1908 the Castle's watersheds were designated part of the larger Rocky Mountain Forest Reserve that extended along the Eastern Slopes north from the u.s. border.

Public land, now bordered by private land and defined by new government boundaries, was no longer connected to the historic ebb and flow of indigenous hunter/gatherers or a fur trade economy. The Castle was now a defined reserve. Intense resource consumption replaced more sustainable land-use practices. Legal documents and bureaucratic language began to replace traditional knowledge and local stories. The particular needs of each competing economic interest narrowed the definition and discourse of land use even further. For the rancher the Castle meant grass; for the farmer downstream it represented water; for the hunter it was game; for the logger, trees; for the miner, coal; for the developer, real estate.

With each user group came the desire to control rights and access to resources, and the government, with few restrictions, yielded. Even as water sources were being protected on paper, the resources that constitute healthy watersheds were being divvied up on the ground. Any notion of public lands for the common good could now be chopped up and literally carted away.

During the early years of European settlement southwestern Alberta's mountain forests were in little jeopardy of overuse, although the stage was set. The Castle was more a backdrop for significant resource extraction and development. Relatively few people other than trappers, outfitters and range riders actually used the more remote mountain valleys. Settlers, other than taking the occasional hunting trip, were working too hard and too close to home as they established themselves on the prairies and in the foothill valleys. Even with the Castle region's first grist and saw mill established up Mill Creek Valley in 1879 and the completed Crowsnest Pass railway in 1898, which utilized a large volume of local lumber, forests deep in the Castle remained largely untouched.

Following the u.s. initiative to preserve public lands through a National Park system, which began with Yellowstone in 1872, Canada began its own series of park designations with Banff in 1885. In southern Alberta, Waterton Forest Park – then a tiny 140-square-kilometre refuge – was redesignated in 1911. Often seen as a mountain playground for the local population, Waterton Lakes National Park was boldly expanded three years later to add all of the Rocky Mountain Forest Reserve south of the Carbondale River.[6] Grazing, trapping, outfitting and hunting were allowed to continue inside the park boundaries, and for a time the future looked bright for the Castle and its watersheds.

Unfortunately, this union would not last past the seven-year itch, as disagreements over wildlife and resource management between Forestry and the National Park System intensified. The Castle was removed from the park in 1921, once again becoming part of the federal Forest Reserve, while Waterton Lakes National Park shrank back to nearly its present-day size of 505-square-kilometre. The retrenchment from National Park back to Forest Reserve probably had little immediate bearing on the day-to-day existence of the Castle, but it would have a significant impact in the years to come as control over the Castle shifted and the demand for its resources increased.

---

6        With its emergent coal mining industry, and with the First World War at hand, the Crowsnest Pass was kept out of any park expansion plans.

By 1928 the South and West Castle valleys were being logged for more than just local services. In 1929 an oil well was drilled at the bottom of Haig Ridge. Seismic activity began the same year and although temporarily scaled back during the Depression the search for oil and gas would return in earnest during the Second World War. Then, in 1930, the federal government transferred control of the Rocky Mountain Forest Reserve and its resources to the province. Viewed from the present time, perhaps no management decision would be more critical for the future of the Castle. Now under provincial jurisdiction, it was to be managed as a game preserve while other resources – logging, grazing, oil and gas exploration – continued unabated.

Almost daily testimony of the great potential hidden wealth in the form of natural gas and petroleum as well as metallic minerals of great value awaiting exploration and development, ... this hidden wealth will be uncovered and converted for the benefit of these three provinces and their people. Some of these deposits have already been developed and

In 1929 an exploration oil well was drilled at the base of Haig Ridge in the West Castle valley. A support camp for the well was set up along the West Castle River further downstream, along Hwy. 774 at the Castle Falls Road junction. To the left is well-known guide and photographer Bert Riggall. Photo courtesy of the Kootenai Brown Pioneer Village and Pincher Creek Historical Society.

others are being turned into production, but even in these known fields
cumulative evidence points to the probability that only the surface has
been scratched ... In this great search for new wealth ... the advance of
scientific knowledge is destined to play an increasingly important role
and will probably hasten the day when much of this hidden wealth will
be uncovered ...

— *Pincher Creek Echo* editorial, August 20, 1936

In 1936 a massive forest fire burned some 700,000 acres of land in Montana,
Alberta and British Columbia, including the West Castle, South Castle
and Carbondale valleys. In the fire's aftermath salvage logging increased
significantly, sparing little of the forest's natural regeneration. By the early
1940s logging throughout the Castle was beginning to have noticeable
impacts on the rivers and resident trout populations. Even though hunting
had been banned, certain wildlife populations were declining while others
fluctuated wildly. Meanwhile oil and gas wells were once again being drilled.
Grass was being over-grazed. Horse trails that once followed indigenous
trails were turning into roads while seismic lines were becoming the new
routes into the Castle's backcountry.

Within a generation the Castle had become a marquee tent in a
three-ring resource circus complete with an environmental high-wire
act. The main thrust behind the 1908 designation and management of
Crown land – to protect the environmental quality of the region's vital
watersheds – was in jeopardy. Too many private interests were carving
into the Castle with little or no regard for the specific and cumulative
impacts on water quality and wildlife habitat. The growing conflicts
around land-use allocation throughout the 90,000-square-kilometre
Eastern Slopes Forest Reserve was now a major cause for concern. The
Alberta government of the day, in a moment of clarity, decided a new,
coordinated management strategy was in order to rein in the damage.

In 1947 the Alberta and Canadian governments signed a 25-year
agreement that established the joint Eastern Rockies Forest Conservation
Board. The two governments laid out a framework for integrated

The discovery of oil in Waterton Lakes National Park led to seismic activity and exploration drilling along the Front Range to the north, including Yarrow Creek, seen here in 1919–1920. The oil reserves proved to be insignificant, and as the Depression set in, seismic and drilling activity in and around the Castle shut down. The rediscovery of gas reserves with the 1957 Discovery Well in Pincher Canyon led to the drilling of 50 wells in the Front Range alone. Even as rumours of a declining reserve ciculate, new wells continue to be drilled in the Castle. Photo by Bert Riggall, courtesy of the Kootenai Brown Pioneer Village and Pincher Creek Historical Society.

resource management where individual industries could not operate without considering the cumulative impacts on the environment. In 1948, the Board launched its "Green Area" initiative, which prohibited residential development and agricultural use other than grazing in the Forest Reserve. Of primary concern and focus for the Board was the "environmental degradation and consequent risks of flooding that resulted from uncoordinated logging in the Eastern Slopes" (Kennett, 4). Even so, logging continued unabated.

Over the years, the Eastern Rockies Forest Conservation Board's effectiveness weakened steadily as the Alberta government took control of resource development. In 1954 the Castle's status as a Provincial Game Reserve was rescinded. The provincial government, stepping over the Board, subdivided public lands into forestry management units which they could control themselves under the Alberta Forest Service. This move undercut the Board's authority to issue resource use permits and further reduced its role to overseeing minor policy tasks and the coordination of research and watershed monitoring projects.

The Castle and the rest of the Eastern Slopes faced a regular dose of revised government schemes and policy shifts as the Board's power steadily declined. Without strong management, special interests continued to rule the day over resources as the quality of the Castle's natural environments declined. It was a government-led war of attrition against conservation in Alberta at a time when the u.s. was recognizing the need to protect wilderness by passing its landmark Wilderness Act in 1964.

Finally, in 1977, after two years of public consultation and another two years of review, Peter Lougheed's recently elected Conservative provincial government replaced the once heralded but now defunct Forest Conservation Board with their own Public Lands & Wildlife department and a "*Policy for Resource Management of the Eastern Slopes.*"

Public Lands & Wildlife introduced three principal land use zones into the management equation: protection, resource management, and development. Within these broadly conceived zones eight subzones outlined ranges of permitted activities. Labelling them "prime protection," "critical wildlife" and "special use" all the way down to "industrial" and "facility development," it appeared that the Lougheed government was responding to the issue of watershed and wilderness protection. Instead, the zone designations based on definable ecoregions merely mirrored existing land use and resource extraction. The new policy was in almost every sense a pro-development plan dressed up in green.

Under this system, the "prime protection" designation, which offered the most control over environmental degradation, had its boundaries restricted to the alpine regions of the Castle. The alpine ecoregion, with its thin soil, is by nature fragile but what does exist above treeline is of no use to a sawmill. And what about fragile ecosystems below treeline? Designating Prairie Bluff a "critical wildlife zone" to protect important mountain sheep habitat did not prevent Shell from planning and eventually drilling a series of sour-gas wells on the mountain's slopes. The unconscious formula labelled already extensively logged regions in the greater Carbondale watershed as "multiple use." Even with a new resource management policy in the hands of government it remained business as usual in the Castle.

Seven years later the policy was revised, but "reflecting the realities of the economic situation in Alberta," the 1984 version did little to protect watersheds or critical wildlife habitats and instead continued to stress the benefits of development:

> The Policy is sufficiently flexible so that all future proposals for land
> use and development may be considered. No legitimate proposals
> will be categorically rejected. Should a proposal not be in keeping
> with the provisions of the Policy for that area, alternative means will
> be explored for accommodating the proposal in a more appropriate
> location in the region.
>
> — Hon. Don Sparrow, Associate Minister, Public Lands & Wildlife, in
> "A Policy for Resource Management of the Eastern Slopes, Revised 1984"

Caught in the free-fall of revisions, areas like Jutland Brook deep in the South Castle were removed from their "prime protection" status, while other restrictions were relaxed, precipitating the go-ahead to drill the Prairie Bluff wells in 1987.

The *Castle River Sub-Regional Integrated Resource Plan,* yet another government policy document, recognized the shifting emphasis toward development, especially the expansion "of a strong tourist industry and for greater recreation development by the private sector." Integrated resource planning slick with oblique bureaucratic jargon continued to be, as a Natural Resources Conservation Board (NRCB) report put it, "a key mechanism for the provision of opportunities to ensure the integrity of the original Eastern Slopes Policy is maintained." The government was providing more incentives for development rather than addressing the increasing negative pressures on the land. The culmination of over 40 years of integrated management, it appeared, amounted to nothing more than the justification of its own bureaucratic survival with the emphasis on development over its fundamental and oh-so-long-ago objective of watershed protection.

## Waterton-Castle Wildland Recreation Area and the NRCB decision

*"... the Board has reviewed the state of the Crown of the Continent Ecosystem and its subregions with particular emphasis on the Waterton-Castle Area. The Board reached a qualitative conclusion that the Crown of the Continent Ecosystem is at risk and that the Waterton Castle Area in particular has deteriorated. It also concluded that without coordinated action on the part of the numerous agencies with jurisdiction over parts of the Crown Ecosystem, the deterioration would continue to the detriment of the ecosystem and those who use it."*

— Natural Resources Conservation Board report, December 1993

In between the implementation of each Act, policy and plan there were the endless studies, public round tables and stakeholder meetings, even small pockets of active resistance. People were tired. The land was tired. Expansion, contraction, extraction had taken their toll on the Castle and the surrounding communities. By the 1990s it was clear that the Alberta government's integrated resource management schemes were failing to meet their objectives. The damage to the environment was so clear by this time that in its review of a major proposal to convert the existing community-run ski hill in the West Castle Valley into a privately owned four-season tourist destination the provincially appointed NRCB acknowledged the Castle had deteriorated significantly and that the greater Crown of the Continent was at risk.

For a region struggling economically the resort was seen as a possible saviour and many locals encouraged approval of it. Others, concerned about the continuing exploitation of Alberta's natural resources at the expense of wilderness, were cautiously optimistic of the NRCB process. At least most agreed there would be the opportunity for public input on an actual development proposal and not just on another meaningless government policy change. How the Board responded to the ski hill expansion plans would go a long way in determining the province's commitment to protecting public land and its commitment to preserving the Castle.

In the fall of 1993, after presiding over a summer of public hearings, the NRCB stated that the resort was acceptable if two critical conditions were met: that the project be redesigned to reduce its impact on the environment; and that a large protected area surrounding the·development be designated to offset the impact of the resort. The NRCB proposed a "Waterton-Castle Wildland Recreation Area" that would extend from present-day Waterton Lakes National Park to the park's former northern boundary – what amounted to most of the public Forest Reserve south of the municipality of Crowsnest. By adopting the original boundaries of the extended Waterton Lakes National Park the recommendation for a wildland area was the most promising turn in the bitter debate that had played out during the public consultation.

When I moved to Pincher Creek in 1994 many locals were displaying signs reading "This business supports ski hill expansion." Others publicly opposed development through letters and coalition organizing. One longtime resident even went so far as to describe Pincher Creek to me as "the crisis capital of Canada." No fewer than 86 separate presentations were made to the NRCB, an incredible demonstration of local diversity and division unprecedented in the history of the region and a long way from any idea of the Castle as a common landscape. The fragmentation of the Castle into special interests was of critical concern and the NRCB's recommendation was seen as a constructive way to unite public opinion and protect the Castle once and for all.

A 12-person stakeholder group was established to help define the limits of use and protection within the designated Waterton-Castle Wildland Recreation Area. With some goodwill and effort southern Alberta could get an expanded ski resort *and* a significant wildland area and the Castle could well return to a modern version of its old self.

Unfortunately no deal was struck. The multistakeholder group lasted just long enough for animosities to arise and effectively kill the process. To be fair, the majority of stakeholders had agreed in principle on user restrictions in Waterton-Castle Wildland Recreation Area. The logging industry and motorized recreational vehicle users and Shell Canada, however, held out for the status quo. This was enough of a stalemate for the government to pull the plug on the NRCB's decision.

With the Castle's future at stake it has proved incredibly difficult to talk across special-interest and ideological boundaries, especially when historical and political perspectives toward public lands have encouraged division and not cooperation. Such dialogue is nearly impossible when government does not respect the recommendations of its own regulatory bodies such as the NRCB or the public's good faith in consultation. When the government of Alberta declined to meet the terms for a wildland recreation area, the project application was withdrawn and in 1995 the NRCB moved on to review other projects. In the spring of that year a massive flood, larger than any other witnessed in the previous 100 years, burst out from the Castle and battered southern Alberta.

## Flood of the Century

Each time I hike into the Pincher Creek headwaters I stop at a small waterfall a few kilometres from the trailhead for a snack and water break. It is here that the trail turns up and away from Pincher Creek and into a side valley before continuing on to Victoria Ridge. Watching a water ouzel flit about in the cooling spray, it is hard to picture the creek differently when the spring rains come and the snow melts and it takes on a personality of a different sort. It is even harder to imagine the torrent that surged down one day in 1995 at a rate 200 times greater than what I was witnessing on a quiet summer's day ten years and a month later.

Back then I was eagerly anticipating an event-filled summer covering the Waterton Lakes and Glacier National Parks regional news for the *Waterton-Glacier Views*. It was June 5. I was only one week on the beat and it was raining. Raining really hard. Word was that with so much snow still in the mountains the downpour could push creeks, already swollen with spring meltwater, over the edge. All I could do was make a few phone calls and watch stunned from our second-floor office window as thick trees and dark mud hurtled down Pincher Creek.

South of town, just east of the Castle Wilderness along North Drywood Creek, Janet Main and Charlie Straessle were also watching the rain. They were concerned the Shell Waterton gas plant dam that

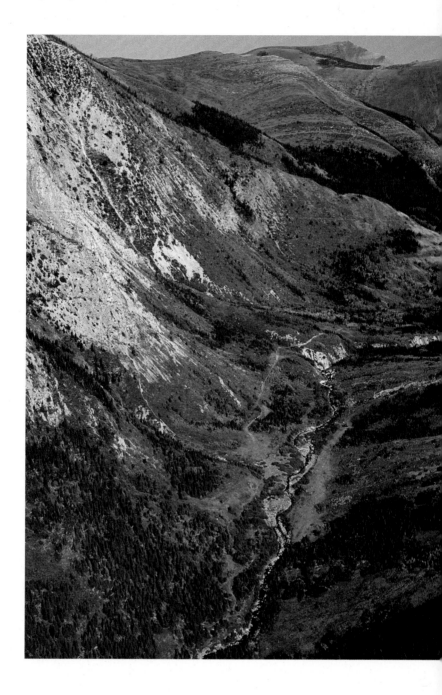

crossed upstream from their ranch might break, and they were frantically tying down the sheds and equipment in their barnyard. Throughout the municipal districts of Pincher Creek and Crowsnest Pass similar scenarios were playing out. Many people took stock, battened down the hatches and prepared for the worst. Others made phone calls. Meanwhile, the rain kept falling, the snow kept melting and the water kept rising.

By early afternoon what was once only a threat became very real. The creek banks surrendered and water rushed over the land. In Pincher Creek, Bridge Avenue's namesake structure collapsed. Dozens of other bridges throughout the district washed away and many more threatened to yield. Sections of road caved in. Sandbag dikes gave way. Houses were swamped. Barnyards became rushing rivers; pastures, small lakes. Cattle drowned. Even the Oldman Reservoir, modern engineering's promise of local flood control and downstream irrigation, couldn't handle the volume flowing out of the Castle and off the fields.

As the flood approached its peak the remote weather-monitoring station up the Pincher Creek headwaters had already clocked 300 mm of rain, a third of its yearly total precipitation, in less than 24 hours. A little to the northwest the Castle River's instantaneous discharge was double its previous recorded maximum. Twenty million gallons of water were pouring into the Oldman Reservoir every minute. This wasn't just a pickup truck full of water constantly slamming into the reservoir every second, it was more a semi-trailer load. Operators for the first time in the Oldman Dam's short history were forced to release the massive overflow onto the largely unsuspecting communities and residents downstream. It was no wonder, then, that as Janet and Charlie looked on from the safety of high ground the Shell dam burst, sending a wall of water over their land. It was, they say, a flood for the century.

But it wasn't the only flood over the past hundred years. With over half of the Castle's annual volume of water flowing between mid-May and mid-July, any combination of heavy rain, warm temperatures and

Aerial view of Pincher Creek, looking downstream in the fall when water levels are typically at their lowest. Victoria Peak is in the background. Photo courtesy of Lorne Fitch.

lingering snowpack can cause havoc in the flatlands. In normal years, excess water is contained in the streams, rivers, sloughs and lakes or is absorbed by the soil and plants. Often these are pushed to the limit. There were, after all, the floods of 1908, 1923, 1937, 1953, 1964 and 1975. But the residents of Pincher Creek had yet to see anything quite like 1995. The record rainfall on June 5 took care of that. (Ten years later, Pincher Creek was again on high flood alert. This time the town was spared, as heavy flooding occurred 160 kilometres to the north, along the Highwood River.)

**After the Flood**

The ritual of the spring flood has been a principal force of renewal in the Castle as long as there have been mountains and rivers, snowmelt and rains. Creek banks erode; cut-off channels materialize; trees and shrubs get uprooted. The last flood's log and boulder jams are carried away, only to be replaced by new ones somewhere else. Water bursts banks and swirls over the valley bottoms, leaving a mess of rock, sand, mud and lumber. To the eager, unappreciative hiker, floods merely wash away trails and block access. To the unsuspecting eye much looks destroyed. Wreckage from the 1995 flood is still visible on many routes in the lower reaches of the South Castle.

Within the flood-torn ruins there are seeds of renewal. Flush with natural nutrients, the Castle's floodplains, forests and wetlands are reinvigorated. As the water subsides, lingering ponds and puddles squirm with aquatic life. Amphibians dormant through the winter – maybe even since the last flood – awaken and lay their eggs. Gravel bars and cowbellies[7] once choked with fine silt and decaying vegetation are flushed out, leaving fresh spawning grounds for trout. This organic drift becomes food for the

Drywood Creek after the floodwaters of June 1995 began to recede. Photo courtesy of Lorne Fitch.

---

7        Old term for places along the banks of slow-moving creeks where the current slackens and the finest particles settle into a silt so plush it is said to be "soft like a Holstein's belly" (Lopez & Gwartney 2006).

plankton-eaters downstream – insect larvae, crustaceans and fish – in a rush of productivity that reaches well into the prairies, a phenomenon known as the "flood pulse" (Savage).

Too much disturbance, however, can disrupt this sequence. Development, roads, logging, grazing – all potentially interfere with a watershed's natural capacity to control flooding. They can erode a stream bank's structural integrity, weaken its ability to hold the rush of water, and contribute excessive amounts of sediment and debris into the flow. Further downstream, farmers and ranchers getting a jump on the growing season are busy tilling, planting and fertilizing. Fertilizer applied just before a heavy rain is apt to go into the creek and not the soil. Those that work the land are aware of this but no one can summon favourable weather when it's most appropriate. It's often a case of taking advantage of today's window of blue sky rather than holding off until later on the strength of nothing more than tomorrow's hollow promise of rain. And depending on the quality of farmers' creeks, a little or a lot of erosion occurs. Supercharged with mud and manure the flood pulse can pack a wallop.

Nineteen ninety-five was a watershed year for the Castle. Out of the debris from the flood and the failure around the NRCB decision, besides damage and disappointment came a renewed consciousness: nature here is not only unpredictable but also vulnerable.

## The Castle Today, The Castle Tomorrow: Reimagining and Restoring Wilderness

*Like many wilderness areas hanging in the balance, especially those close to established communities and with different stakeholders laying claim to its resources, the Castle is probably known more for its political battles than for its mountains, valleys, lakes and rivers – disputes and hearings garnering more attention than the wildlife and unique plants to be discovered. Its history buried under piles of logged timber. Its diverse culture scarred by seismic lines and roads.*

— Journal entry, November 2005

In 1997, with the area still recouping, I attended a preliminary meeting for the Yellowstone to Yukon Conservation Initiative at the community hall in Waterton Lakes National Park. Back then, Y2Y, as it is known, was in its infancy, an ambitious concept to connect existing protected areas – parks, forest reserves and wilderness areas like the Castle – with wildlife corridors from Yellowstone National Park north to the Yukon. Pincher Creek, Alberta, lies within Y2Y's theoretical boundaries, of course, and one day I got a call at the *Waterton-Glacier Views* office from a friend and old university roommate, Karsten Heuer.[8] He told me I should drop in on the meeting and check it out.

Much of Y2Y's success hinges on getting protection for the Castle, the narrowest and most vulnerable part in the whole scheme. National parks were not nearly enough to preserve wildlife into the future, conservation biologists were saying. Lose the Castle and you lose the ability to support large, roaming carnivores in the southernmost parts of Y2Y. Grizzly bears and wolves south of the 49th parallel would effectively be cut off from the Rocky Mountain spine to the north, part of their historical range, isolating them in pockets of habitat now known to be too small to ensure their natural survival. The importance of getting the Castle protected was not lost on members of the Castle-Crown Wilderness Coalition, a relatively small but active environmental group based in Pincher Creek. Grander schemes aside, the ccwc had been advocating hard for protection of the Castle in its own right since 1990.

After the meeting I joined three others at the local Thirsty Bear Saloon. It would have been hard to find myself in more powerful company when it came to advocating for protection for the Castle: Gordon Petersen, a Beaver Mines resident, wildlife photographer and president of the ccwc; Mike Sawyer, an unrelenting, often confrontational environmental consultant from Calgary who was to become the coordinator for the ccwc's strategic campaign in the late 1990s; and Mike Judd, a lifetime area resident and local outfitter, an iconoclast who had probably done more to raise public

---

8      Between June 1998 and September 1999 Heuer hiked, skied and canoed 3,400 km of Rocky Mountain spine from Yellowstone National Park in Wyoming to Watson Lake in the Yukon. The journey is chronicled in his book *Walking the Big Wild: From Yellowstone to Yukon on the Grizzly Bear's Trail.*

awareness and gained more media attention regarding the Castle than any other individual. Mike's tactics were unusually daring, and to some, foolhardy, interventions and blockades that possibly turned as many people off as not. Pushing emotional, philosophical and political buttons was necessary business. For these three the stakes were high.

As for me, I wasn't sure where I sat. The battle scars within and surrounding the Castle were obvious, but the landscape itself was still largely unknown to me. I'd only lived here for three years. Even though I had done some hikes, attended some meetings, reported on a number of the issues, even taken on ccwc stewardship responsibilities for one of the trails, I was still getting my feet wet.

I attempted to debate the merits of public inclusion and compromise, arguing you couldn't put a lock and key on the Castle, not when local people's lives historically depended on its natural resources. Petersen, Sawyer and Judd would have no part of this argument. For them the time for compromise was over. The NRCB's recommendation to establish a protected area, the most promising outcome of the debate around the ski resort expansion, had failed and a precipitous freefall into further disruptive resource extraction and development loomed. The ski hill was quietly hatching a new expansion plan, wide swaths near the Goat Creek headwaters were being logged, sour gas pipelines were rupturing while others were being built, and fresh seismic activity was just around the corner. My arguments got hammered like horseshoes.

Ten years on, some things have changed. Ralph Klein's provincial reign, first as environment minister and then as premier, is over, his "Special Places 2000" initiative[9] and its illusions of environmental protection for the Castle all but in the shredder. West Castle ski hill is now Castle Mountain Resort and with the name change come the incremental effects of the grander tourist destination – more ski runs, more lifts, chalets and hostels. Other things have changed little. Random camping clogs the

9        In 1992 the Alberta government tabled a draft policy aimed at protecting representative areas of environmental significance throughout the province by 2000. The final Special Places draft was released in 1995 and the public was encouraged to nominate areas. By 2001, 81 new and 13 expanded sites totalling two million hectares had been added to Alberta's parks and protected areas land base. The Castle is the only Special Places nominee that did not receive any kind of formal protection.

lower valleys, and motorized vehicles continue to tear around the trails and logging roads more or less unchecked. Local residents continue to fight sour gas wells in their backyards. Logging plans continue to loom heavy over the forest. The plants, the animals, the land struggle to endure.

# Home in the Castle:
# Living on the Margins

Walking through a wind-rattled forest, wandering into an alpine meadow crazy in bloom or cresting a ridge that almost touches the sky can be overwhelming. It is the unsettling but wonderful sensation that you are in a land somewhere other than where you started. You're "not in Kansas anymore," as the saying goes, and depending on how long one takes to the trail or how far one goes, this magical feeling of displacement can happen often. But if it is the land – the trees, the flowers, the rock – that liberates us first and frequently; it is the glimpse of something alive, moving, a fleeting moment of wildness that makes the heart skip and sets you down profoundly in wilderness.

Together with Waterton Lakes National Park, the Castle holds the greatest diversity of animals in Alberta. Fifty-nine species of mammals inhabit the region. An estimated 150 species of birds breed here. The Castle provides a home for several animals at risk of extinction in Alberta: the red-tailed chipmunk, the vagrant shrew, lynx, mountain lions, grizzly bears and wolverines are examples of species living on the edge. The Castle also provides critical winter and summer range for elk, moose, bighorn sheep, mountain goats and mule and white-tailed deer. With such a tally it would appear things are good in the Castle.

During the summer of 2005 I witnessed a wildflower season beyond any in my recent memory. I wound my way through beargrass-choked meadows along the Continental Divide; struggled to stay on the trail through lush, post-fire ground cover up Goat Creek. On Victoria Ridge I came across a vibrant, late-season meadow of shooting star and later hiked through healthy fescue grasses up Spionkop. For sure I was not in Kansas. Yet for all my days on the trail I saw less wildlife than I would ever have imagined and it was unsettling. After years of filming wolves for nature films, Lois Crisler wrote: "Wilderness without animals is dead ... animals without wilderness are a closed book."

## Large Carnivores

> *"Man, through most of his recent evolution from primitive to present-day civilization, has chosen to fight the wilderness blindly, attempting to break nature to his needs, at war with it and sometimes mercilessly destroying the very things he needs the most. The grizzly can show us something of what it means to live in harmony with nature."*
>
> — Andy Russell in *Grizzly Country*

Harmony and eventually marriage brought me to write much of this book from California, home of the UCLA Bruins and the Cal State Golden Bears. The grizzly bear is the State animal. Its image is on the State flag. Bears rule here. There's a billboard advertising a major American financial institution – Bank of the West – that I pass on my daily East Bay commute. The massive head of a grizzly dominates the sign. It is a singularly powerful image. The caption simply states "Since 1874," presumably the year the bank was founded. It could well read "Extinct since 1922." That was the year the last wild grizzly in California was shot and killed. Lesson learned? Today the grizzly is protected from hunting in the U.S., but not in Canada.

Strong conservation arguments on both sides of the border, like

 those presented by the Y2Y concept, emphasize the need for large carnivores such as grizzlies to exist into the future if ecosystems

Conservation arguments on both sides of the border emphasize the need for large carnivores like black bears and grizzlies to exist into the future if the Crown of the Continent ecosystem is to maintain any degree of its natural state.

like the Crown of the Continent are to maintain any degree of their natural state. Bears, wolves, cougars and wolverines, by feeding from the top of the food chain, determine much of an ecosystem's diversity, its composition and its ability to resist destructive forces. Losing keystone predators like the grizzly could ultimately impact the species they feed upon, which can affect other natural characteristics – vegetation and wildfires, for example – effects that will play out to the detriment of the Castle into the future.

But the Castle is not alone. The fact that large carnivores are at risk here is part of a bigger, worldwide problem. Large carnivores are limited even under natural conditions. Most have also had their habitat degraded or fragmented and many remain the target of excessive hunting and poaching. It is not surprising, then, that 65 species in the order *Carnivora* are globally threatened, endangered or at risk (Nabhan, 270).

## Grizzly Bears

The Castle still helps to sustain grizzlies, but only barely. Grizzlies require large home ranges of relatively undisturbed wilderness, up to three times the size of the Castle, and with each major human disturbance the Castle's ability to contribute to the survival of these bears diminishes. How many grizzlies exist here is unclear and is often disputed between those who see grizzlies as necessary and those who deem them dangerous pests. Many of the bears prefer to pass through, or are short-time residents from somewhere else in the Crown of the Continent ecosystem. A local rancher recently told me I wasn't seeing bears in the mountains because they were all out in the ranchland. That may be. The good news is that this was someone who understood and appreciated the need for grizzlies.

Historically, the far-ranging grizzly was abundant throughout southern Alberta. Lewis and Clark in 1805 and Palliser in 1857 reported grizzlies on the Plains. Some researchers have begun to consider the prairie coulees as the bears' preferred habitat. Fifty years ago it would not have been uncommon to spot more than one grizzly in the lower Castle River area during the spring or in the river valleys east of the Front Ranges. Today they are rarely seen. As habitat has been diminished by human development, so have the bears' numbers. Still, the Castle provides habitat to help the Crown of the Continent ecosystem maintain the largest population of non-coastal grizzly bears in North America. The South Castle and West Castle valleys also provide critical passageways through the Rocky Mountains, allowing grizzlies to move back and forth in pursuit of prey between Glacier National Park in Montana and Banff National Park.

But existing habitat and corridors within the Castle are clearly not enough, and what remains is under constant threat. In 1993 Alberta's Natural Resources Conservation Board concluded that "grizzly bear subpopulations in the u.s. and southern Canadian Rocky Mountains are too small for long-term survival without exchanges between them and subpopulations to the north." Since 1950, viable habitat for grizzlies in the Castle has been reduced significantly from road development and increased industrial and recreational traffic.

## Black Bears

A black bear's movement within the Castle is largely determined by its eating habits. Depending where it emerges from its winter den, a black bear might find the carcass of a deer or elk in the lower montane or feed on bearberries in the subalpine. They've even been known to climb poplars to feed on the sprouting new buds. As spring takes hold they seek fresh wetland sedges and dandelions in open areas and along roadsides.

During the heat of the summer black bears typically stay in the forest, overturning logs and tearing apart stumps looking for insects and grubs. Berries on the more open slopes are a staple during late summer and into fall. In years when berry crops are poor, which can often be the case in the Castle because of its ever-changing weather, black bears will wander far and wide and onto private land and into campgrounds looking for food.

Although they are not as sensitive to human activity as grizzly bears are, black bears too are threatened by the loss of habitat. Road development, off-road vehicles, conflicts with humans and in particular hunting are threatening the black bear's survival in the Castle.

## The Saga of Wolves in the Castle

*Wolves have long been reduced to a symbol of wilderness. They adorn T-shirts and logos. Local gift shops and art galleries sell all likeness and unlikeness of them – on jewellery, as cheap trinkets and stuffed toys, in carvings and on canvases. Whether you think the "art" is good or bad, it's an odd place for the wolf to end up – as a caricature, an aesthetic misrepresentation, an apology from a society that's largely lost its connection to things wild.*

— Journal entry, January 2007

*"Then I saw the wolf, no more than a smudge of jerky movement, edging its way across a meadow hundreds of metres below. Its stop-and-go motion caught my eye, minutes of stillness followed by explosive leaps and bounds. I leaned into a rock to steady my binoculars."*

— Karsten Heuer, *Walking the Big Wild*

I have been lucky to have seen a number of wolves. These sighting, however, were mostly up in Alaska, the Northwest Territories and northern Saskatchewan. While working as a ranch hand on the edge of the Castle I witnessed a pregnant heifer's hindquarters torn to shreds by wolves, the muscle hanging ragged and putrefied (both cow and calf lived). But like Heuer I have witnessed only one wolf within the Castle. The year was 1994. I too only caught a "smudge," a few seconds of black, hastening across a snowbound bowl.

Wolves, however, were once abundant throughout southern Alberta, so much so that the early fur traders constantly noted their presence among the herds of bison. But it was a richness soon to be robbed from the land. Wolves began their decline with the killing off of the buffalo and the overhunting of elk and deer by settlers. Without their prey, wolves were hard-pressed to survive. Poisoning them for their fur, known as "wolfing," killed thousands more. Then, in 1899, a wolf bounty was introduced in southern Alberta. With the Western Stock Growers' Association underwriting the bounty, it is estimated another 2,800 wolves were killed over the next ten years.

The pressure on wolves continued and was relentless. More livestock kills in the neighbouring ranchland forced park officials' hands and the last wolves were removed from Waterton Lakes National Park in 1922. With the wolf population in decline, elk (at the time there were only about 400 in all of Alberta) recovered dramatically. Deer, moose and bighorn sheep increased as well. However, even with the increase in their prey, wolves responded poorly. Some moved in from northern Alberta and British Columbia. With pelts no longer in high demand and the bounty occasionally withdrawn, wolves made a minor comeback by the end of the 1940s.

But the recovery was short-lived. Ranchers reported more livestock kills; hunters and wildlife managers complained of low ungulate numbers. In 1951 wolf snares were legalized and cyanide distributed. Control even resumed in the national parks, and it is estimated that from 1952 to 1956 thousands of wolves were killed. For the second time since early settlement, the wolf in Alberta, especially in the Castle, was at a low point. The few sightings, combined with known shootings, barely confirmed their presence in the area.

After a long absence from southern Alberta, wolves reappeared in 1992. In 1993 the first documented den in the area since the 1950s was located in Waterton Lakes National Park. Over the next two years it was estimated that 50–60 wolves ranged through the Castle between the u.s. border and Banff National Park. Two smaller packs became established, one near Beauvais Lake Provincial Park, the other along the Carbondale River.

Meanwhile, the provincial government was reducing the funds available to compensate ranchers for livestock killed or injured by predation. In 1994 a meeting held at the Twin Butte Community Hall, south of Pincher Creek, launched a new, privately funded livestock compensation program into the area. Later that year, after a series of livestock killings and maulings, hunters killed most of the wolves, despite the efforts of local ranchers, conservationists, national park wardens and provincial wildlife officers to support the new program.

## Other Carnivores

Marten, fishers, lynx, cougar and wolverine all require what remains of the Castle's undisturbed mature forests. Of all these forest carnivores, the marten appears to be faring the best. It once appeared that the fisher was gone from the Castle, but in 1991 biologists located fisher tracks in the West Castle Valley. The wolverine is one of the rarest carnivores in the Rockies. Seldom seen, they avoid all things human. Off-road vehicles in the alpine, especially snowmobiles, are not a welcome sight. While you might never see a wolverine during your hikes, if you are in the alpine and there is still snow, there is a chance you might see their tracks. Bobcats and cougar, also naturally wary of humans, are rarely spotted.

By 1997 fewer than 15 wolves survived south of the Crowsnest Pass. Today most wolves in the Castle are like the lone individuals Karsten Heuer and I witnessed, just passing through.

## Ungulates

The Castle, and the Front Ranges in particular, were once considered one of the best bighorn sheep habitats in North America. A 2002 survey accounted for over 280 bighorn sheep in the Castle, with the Front Ranges still being the most desired habitat. Two major die-offs from bronchial disease during the 20th century, however, caused bighorn populations in the Castle to plummet. During the latest outbreak, in 1982–1983, almost half succumbed

Wolverine tracks high on Three Lakes Ridge.

101

to disease. While bighorn sheep in other areas have rebounded, the population in the Castle's Front Ranges have not regained their original numbers. Some have speculated there is a connection between their slow return and oil and gas exploration in the Front Range canyons, but the science is inconclusive.

The number of elk in the Castle is not known for certain. By all accounts it has dropped significantly from the more than 3,000 estimated in 1953. The snow-free, south-facing slopes of the Front Range canyons in particular provide important winter range. Today three large winter herds totalling over 1,400 gather along the canyons' eastern edge. Along the Castle's northern boundary elk move down from the subalpine meadows through the lower Castle Valley montane and gather on private land around the Beaver Mines and Gladstone Valley areas, as well as in Beauvais Lake Provincial Park.

Whitetail deer are common in the Castle at lower elevations, browsing aspen stands and meadows, while mule deer tend to forage higher up on south-facing grassy slopes. Both deer species are important food sources for wolves, cougars and wolverine. White-tailed deer are known to adapt better to human disturbance and development, whereas mule deer are less tolerant to change. In the past mule deer were more frequent, but today it appears whitetails outnumber them.

Vigilant mule deer along the North Kootenay trail.

Moose were hunted out of the Castle at the end of the 1800s, but they have since returned. From spring through fall moose typically spread throughout the area, using all the Castle's aquatic habitats, including higher-elevation streams and tarns.

## Small Mammals

The Castle is also home to over 30 species of small mammals, including numerous ground squirrels, beaver, pika, snowshoe hare and hoary marmot. The Castle is the only place in the province where the wandering shrew is found, while the rare red-tailed chipmunk has been located only in the subalpine of West Castle Valley and Waterton Lakes National Park.

## Reptiles & Amphibians

When it comes to amphibians and reptiles the Castle has many, but most are considered either sensitive to or at risk of extinction. Of note, the long-toed salamander, the spotted frog and the western toad survive here. Two lesser-known and vanishing reptiles, the plains and wandering garter snakes, also continue to exist.

Their winter range shifts as the winter progresses, varying as well depending on the amount of snowfall. During early winter, until the snow deepens, moose appear in open habitats, including higher-elevation fir and spruce stands. Once the winter is fully settled in, they concentrate themselves in the lower valley bottoms along the main rivers and creeks.

It's estimated over 100 mountain goats inhabit the alpine of the Continental Divide between Waterton Lakes National Park and Highway 3 in the Crowsnest Pass. Once found throughout the Castle, they have disappeared from the Front Ranges and interior ridges. Once goats are gone from an area it takes a long time for them to return naturally. In the late 1990s Alberta Fish &

Western toad, primarily terrestrial, needs healthy aquatic habitat for reproduction.

Wildlife attempted to reintroduce them on Barnaby Ridge, but it was not successful. Many of the goats crossed the West Castle Valley over to Syncline Mountain (a favourite goat haunt) and further on to the ridges of Mount Darrah along the Divide. Others migrated to the northern ridges of Waterton Lakes National Park.

## Birds

Birds are niche experts, and the Castle's physical diversity provides them a variety of habitats. There are roughly 105 species of breeding birds here. The area provides nesting habitat for golden eagles, red-tailed hawks, goshawks, great horned owls and northern pygmy owls. For some species the Castle represents the edge of their range: it is the southernmost limit of the boreal owl and the northernmost limit of the Williams sapsucker and white-throated swift. Wetlands support the uncommon northern water thrush. The reclusive harlequin duck can also be found on the rivers and mountain streams. Other species of interest thought to breed in the Castle are the olive-sided flycatcher, western wood peewee, red-naped sapsucker, Hammond's flycatcher, Swainson's thrush, solitary vireo, warbling vireo,

## Eagle Migration

In the spring of 1992, Peter Sherrington and Des Allen observed a single golden eagle heading northwest, high above the Kananaskis Valley. Mildly curious, by the end of the day they had counted over a hundred golden eagles following the same path. This chance discovery opened a window onto a major eagle migration route. The conventional wisdom had been that only small numbers of young golden eagles migrated through the foothills and certainly none used the higher mountain ridges. Since that single sighting, however, more than 50,000 eagles, both bald and, much more significantly, golden eagles have been recorded along southern Alberta's Eastern Slopes during the popular annual spring and fall migration counts.

The Castle is considered a key funnelling and dispersal area along the eagle migration corridor. From mid-February to mid-May, eagles moving north through many Rocky Mountain ranges begin to collect here, as the mountains ranges narrow significantly over the Crowsnest Pass. On their return flight from mid-September to late November, the eagles use the updrafts along the eastern slopes of the Livingstone Range. After crossing the

Crowsnest River they continue along a series of ridges northwest of Beaver Mines before fanning out again over the Castle, some tracking the more eastern ridges, others following the Continental Divide. On the right day, certain vantage points along the northeastern edge of the Castle can provide front-row seats to the dramatic sight of dozens of eagles, golden and bald, soaring past, one after another after another.

MacGillivray's warbler, Wilson's warbler, black-headed grosbeak and Cooper's hawk.

Another 60 species – thousands upon thousands of individual birds – migrate through. Straddling the eastern edge of the Pacific Flyway and the western edge of the Central Flyway, the Castle and the greater Crown of the Continent are becoming more critical to bird migration as habitat is lost along their margins.

Eagle print in the lingering spring snowpack.

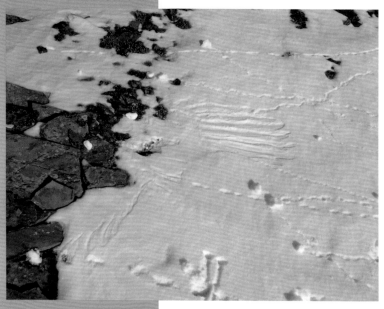

# The Castle's Physical Presence

*"If public retention and management of Western resources was the great conservation theme of the late nineteenth century and preservation of select pieces that of the twentieth, then restoration may well be that of the twenty-first."*

— Dan Flores

Restoring the Castle and the Rocky Mountain West to a "natural state" may indeed become the great North American environmental crusade of the years ahead. If reimagining and then retelling the region's narrative is part of the restoration process, then knowing what the Castle looks like and why will go a long way toward that goal.

Yet, to restore a watershed, an ecosystem, a landscape, we must go beyond just the appearance of our surroundings. To see only scenery hints at a separation between the viewer and the view, where we see only a two-dimensional space, distant, limited and lifeless. Better to seek a third dimension and explore the vegetation and topography along with its wildlife. Still, if this third dimension is only

## Bull Trout

Bull trout have historically fared well in the Castle. Old-time residents recall the streams in the early half of the 1900s teeming with the native fish, a time when catching their daily limit of 25 trout was never a problem. Today bull trout are in serious decline throughout their North American range. Listed as "threatened" in Alberta, they are still found in over 90 per cent of their historical range in the Castle, though their numbers have steadily declined. Gone are the historic "monsters," the fish that helped sustain the Blackfoot as the bison disappeared.

Still prized by anglers, bull trout are now considered an important indicator of aquatic ecosystem health. Like other headwaters fish such as cutthroat trout (also in decline), bull trout need 3°C water — cold, clear and clean. Forestry, off-road vehicle use and to some degree cattle have compromised the quality of water in the Castle. Logging has removed cover, which has increased water temperature in the summer. Streambank erosion from motorized vehicles and cattle, along with excess surface runoff from logged areas, increase siltation, which affects the bull trout's ability to breed and feed.

Cas Main and Andy Russell fishing for bull trout in the Crown of the Continent in 1963. Photo courtesy of the Russell, Main and Freeman families.

defined by attributes and constraints like lakes and rivers, ecosystems and climate, one makes the mistake of appreciating wilderness only with the head and not from the heart, seeing only processes that are distant, limited and soulless.

## Climate

> *When the weather is bad you can't leave; when it is good you don't want to.*
>
> — Local saying

The weather in the Castle is influenced by two opposing air-mass systems: the Pacific Maritime and the Arctic Continental. Warm, moist air from the dominant Pacific system flows over the coastal and interior mountain ranges and collides with the colder Arctic air mass. When the cold Arctic air and warm Pacific air meet, the warmer air rises. This rising air mass, when it reaches dew point, usually brings precipitation.

The dominance of the Pacific Maritime climate has pushed plants and animals that are more common west of the Continental Divide into the Castle. Beargrass and to a lesser extent western hemlock are examples of this trend.[10]

With its distinct wind patterns, the Castle, along with Waterton Lakes National Park, receives Alberta's highest average annual precipitation: 107 cm (42 inches). There is, however, a lot of variability in the area's moisture levels, west to east and south to north. The further from the Continental Divide you go, the drier the climate becomes. Along the Divide deep in the West Castle Valley, precipitation averages 152 cm (60 in.) annually, while along the entrances to the Front Range canyons precipitation falls below 75 cm. Much of the additional precipitation along the Divide is snow, and as a result half of the Castle's annual precipitation falls as snow. And it can snow at any time of the year.

---

10      Recently hikers in the Castle witnessed beargrass in bloom up the North Lost Creek trail, the farthest north in the Castle on record, according to James Tweedie in the *Castle Wilderness News* for August 2007.

Below: The Castle is well known for wind. Sometimes the wind stays at a high enough altitude, just above the ridge tops.
Opposite: Other times gusts can literally knock you off your feet. Photography: Jeff Yee.

Needless to say, with the possibility of snow looming 12 months of the year, the Castle's summers are brief and cool, with an average temperature of 15.3°c from July to mid-August. It can get extremely hot, however, reaching highs in the 30s. Winters are consequently long, but with frequent warm spells brought on by chinooks. The Castle is one of Alberta's warmest places in the winter. Still, temperatures can drop as low as -40oc. Both spring and fall offer some of the most pleasant, if not the most seasonable, weather in the region, although wet, heavy snowstorms in the spring are not uncommon.

Southern Alberta is well known for its winds. The rows and clusters of wind turbines across the region's ranchlands are testaments to its velocity and persistence. Winds in the Castle are predominantly from the southwest and can reach gale force in valleys at any time of the year. The Front Range canyons' east/west valleys funnel these prevailing southwest winds toward the open grasslands, spilling strong, gusty winds out onto the prairie. Windward slopes, scoured bare of snow, become key winter feeding grounds for elk. With an average daily velocity of 30 km/h, a stiff wind is a consistent element of any hike in the Castle, especially along exposed ridges. Many hikers are forced to abandon their high elevation routes as gusts over 100 km/h (60 m.p.h.) are not uncommon and gusts of over 150 km/h (90 m.p.h.) have been recorded.

Adding to the wind factor are the high-cresting airwaves known as chinooks. The Castle averages 28 days of chinook winds during the winter, the highest incidence in Alberta. The average temperature during a chinook is 2.5°c and can be considerably warmer, a welcome relief during the Castle's coldest months, January and February. These stiff, warm winds occur when cool air rapidly falls from the mountain ridges to the prairie. Air moist from its Pacific origins undergoes waves of expansion, cooling and drying as it crosses over the interior mountains toward the prairies. Once past the last of the mountain ridges the air drops onto the grasslands, reaching speeds over 100 km/h, and compresses. For every 100-metre drop in elevation the air temperature increases by one degree Celsius.

Because the Castle has the highest recorded annual precipitation and winter snowfall along the Eastern Slopes, there is a lot of water and it has to go somewhere. Much of it fills the alpine lakes and streams that eventually feed into the Castle River. The Castle itself forms at the confluence of its South Castle and West Castle tributaries. After collecting water from its major tributaries – Lynx and Lost creeks – the Carbondale River joins the Castle just beyond the wilderness boundary. As one of the three major tributaries in the Oldman River ecosystem, the Castle River contributes important moisture to the grasslands and municipalities downstream. But with such high precipitation rates and such dramatic elevation drops over short distances, the Castle's ability to "manage" the flow of moisture is tested every spring during runoff.

**Fire in the Castle**

> *From a modern human perspective, wildfire is usually viewed as a destructive army on the march, threatening property, endangering lives and filling the sky with black, acrid smoke. To our sensibilities, a green forest is a thing of beauty, while a blackened one represents death and ugliness.*
>
> — "Crown of the Continent:
> Profile of a Treasured Landscape"

As wet as most springs can be, and in spite of massively destructive floods like the one in 1995, southern Alberta summers are usually dry. Dry, not wet, is what defines the Eastern Slopes of the Rocky Mountains. The region's relative aridity is why watersheds needed protection in the first place and why healthy forest reserves were considered necessary if settlement were to be successful.

If the southern Alberta landscape is characterized by aridity, fire helps shape it. With ample amounts of ready-made fuel in the form of trees and grass, fires are an inevitable fact of nature. All it takes to start one is a well-placed lightning strike (still the number-one cause of fires throughout the Crown of the Continent) or an idling ATV's hot, sputtering exhaust pipe.

Historical evidence shows a fire burned along the Eastern Slopes once every seven years, an unprecedented frequency along the Rocky Mountain

Leafy arnica and fireweed yet to bloom along Snowshoe Creek Trail. The forest understorey quickly began to return after the Lost Creek Fire of 2003.
Opposite Looking west from a Municipality of Pincher Creek side road. During the "dog days of summer" 2003 the Lost Creek Fire burned out of control for 30 days.

front.[11] Many of these were the result of the indigenous practice of setting fires. These burns renewed the native grasses and kept the spread of willows and potentially dominant aspen and spruce stands to the margins. Of course, whether a fire advances or peters out depends on a number of natural factors, including amount of precipitation, air temperature and prevailing winds. Today the spread of a fire also depends on the fight to suppress it.

---

11        It is estimated that 46 fires greater than 40 hectares in extent occurred between 1633 and 1940: "Waterton Resource Guide," 1997.

Fire has always been a part of the Castle's narrative and each one has a story to tell. Even in the likelihood you did not witness the large wildfires of 1934 or 1936 it is possible to see the charred hulks of white and limber pines up on Whistler Mountain, Barnaby Ridge and Middle Kootenay Pass and imagine those fires' intensity. Fires can also foretell the future. In the summer of 2000 the Cherry Hill fire burned a small section of forest near the heart of the Castle, but it was only a prelude to the inferno that was to come three years later.

**The Lost Creek Fire**

In late July 2003 a small fire started near the Lynx Creek recreation area. For a few minutes at least, until someone in a lookout tower spotted smoke, the fire was out of sight, out of mind. But the flames were far from silent. Fuelled by an excess of tinder-dry vegetation and spread by scorching temperatures, low humidity and swirling mountain winds, this small fire turned into a crackling inferno that burned out of control for 30 days, advancing menacingly onto the doorsteps of the Crowsnest Pass.

Most residents and officials at the time feared the potential loss of property and not the effects on plants and animals as the wildfire came within metres of the towns of Bellevue and Hillcrest. But the anxiety didn't stop the sense of awe. There's an odd combination of wonder that accompanies fear when you can see and breathe impending disaster, even if most of our observations and opinions are made from safe vantage points. Cars lined up along Highway 3 became lounge chairs for drivers turned onlookers. Locals would gather at watering holes like Stella's Bar & Grill in Beaver Mines or the Greenhill Hotel in Blairmore and boldly speculate, over cold beers, about the fire raging just a few kilometres away. Few, save the 1,000 firefighters and dozens of helicopter pilots, could

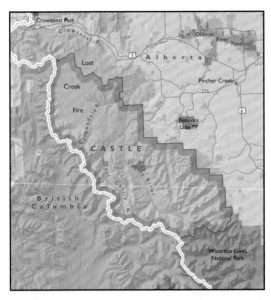

The Lost Creek Fire burned through 51,800 acres, including most of the forest in the northern portion of the Castle.

truly imagine the landscape-altering inferno that was raging in the Castle Wilderness that summer, not even the 2,000 residents that were forced to evacuate their homes, not once but three times.

Trying to contain the fire in the Castle's steep, forested terrain was pretty futile for those on the front line. Whirling dervishes of flame, whipped 10 storeys high within their own firestorms, danced from treetop to treetop or burned deep into the roots. Heat exceeding 1000°c incinerated abandoned camp trailers and bridges. Smoke and ash polluted the air over most of southern Alberta, drifting as far north as Red Deer. More than once flames threatened private property along the south flank of the Crowsnest Pass.

Eventually, favourable winds, aided by well-placed firebreaks and continuous back burning, steered the fire onto rocky ridges and into the dead-end valleys at the base of the Continental Divide. With fuel diminished, the flames began to burn out. By the end of August, with the help of colder temperatures and a late-summer snowfall, the Lost Creek fire was brought under control, though flare-ups continued for another two months. During its devastating run, the fire consumed one-fifth of the Castle: 51,800 acres of forest scorched, thousands of trees burned and an undeterminable amount of wildlife incinerated.

## Choosing Your Battles

*Modern society's effort to extricate fire from the landscape must be viewed as something of an aberration.*

— Stephen Pyne in *Fire: A Brief History*

A hundred and fifty years ago no one was fighting wildfires here like today. Then again, there were no ski resorts, no clusters of houses nestled in the forest, no permanent communities in the river valleys to burn. Timber was not the highly sought-after commodity it has become, and commercial crop production was almost nonexistent. This is not to say that fires historically weren't managed or for that matter mismanaged. There are ample accounts of the Blackfoot and other Plains Indians deliberately setting fires. Fire was used to communicate. Sometimes it was used to instill fear in an adversary's camp or to drive out or trap trespassers. Such fires were often lit and left to burn without much consideration of consequences. Early explorers such as Palliser, seeing acres of grassland scorched before them, were naive in their appreciation of fires that were set deliberately. "Indians ... frequently fire the prairie for the most trivial reasons" (Spry, 75).

Around the Castle, fires were used mostly to improve a group's subsistence, and therefore their outcomes were more measured. Grass burned in the fall and winter would grow earlier in the spring, becoming more lush than in unburned areas, the fresh green grass enticing bison into the area. The burning of fescue grasses along the Front Range in the spring also forced bison out onto the plains, closer to the summer camps. At the same time, it kept the rough fescues off the menu until the fall, luring the bison back to the wintering grounds when the time was ripe. Fires also replenished the soil for other foods such as saskatoon berries and wild prairie turnips (Binnema). These purposely set fires would often take on a life of their own, however, scorching large areas beyond the predetermined boundaries before they burned out naturally.

Fire suppression as we know it began in the early part of the 20th century, around the time the Crown of the Continent was becoming a permanently settled, more intensely managed region. Sparks from cooking fires and from trains along the newly established railways were common fire starters. These fires, in addition to the cycle of natural ones, were no longer considered essential, but instead were now viewed as dangerous and destructive. When a rash of fires swept through the region during the first five years of the new century, a hue and cry arose from the communities and the timber industry. The governments on both sides of the border responded to extinguish the flames of discontent.

Lookout towers were erected to help nip fires in the bud. (In the Castle, the Ironstone and Carbondale lookouts, two of the 128 remaining fire towers in the province, continue to lord it over the Forest Reserve south of Highway 3.) Along with heightened vigilance came an increasingly effective system – crews, equipment and money – for fighting those flames that did get out of hand. Forest management viewed battling wildfires as all-out war and was confident they could be controlled if enough people and materials were brought to bear. By 1950 wildfires in and around the Crown of the Continent were virtually eliminated.

For all this bravado, however, years of fire suppression has set the stage for historically large and destructive fires like Lost Creek by supplying unnatural accumulations of forest fuels ready to burn when conditions are ripe.

This effort to protect human lives, property and resources has also had other, more understated effects on the Castle. Land along the Front Range canyons that has not burned in over 70 years has now shifted from grassland to forest, as invading Douglas firs, willow and alder move in. The loss of native grasses no longer regenerated from seasonal fires forces elk to seek forage in neighbouring pastures and haybales. On high ridges, subalpine fir dominates already threatened indigenous whitebark pine. Preferred winter habitat for bighorn sheep and mule deer has also become crowded with timber.

**Returning to the Scene of the Fire (Some Like It Hot)**

*Like rainfall and wind, natural fires are a basic thread in the fabric of the Crown of the Continent.*

— "Crown of the Continent:
Profiles of a Treasured Landscape"

Wilderness responds differently to fire than humans do. Although often destructive, wildfires are as important as rain and snow, sun and wind when it comes to determining the communities of plants and animals in the Castle. Many species are custom-made for fire. Lodgepole pine trees require intense heat before their cones can open and their seeds disperse. Huckleberries also need high temperatures to regenerate, fire providing fresh openings and rejuvenated soil within its subalpine forest habitat. The Clark's nutcracker uses burned areas to cache whitebark and limber pine seeds, unsuspectingly ensuring the trees' survival as well as the birds' own. Other animals too, most notably black bears and grizzlies, elk and moose, prefer the variety of successive vegetation in fire-created habitats. Lewis's and black-backed woodpeckers, both now rare in southern Alberta, nest in burned-out trees. All are vital signs of life in a blackened landscape. Whether revitalizing fescue grasses, clearing competitors from crowded habitat, popping open seed cones or leaving nutrient-rich ashes to seep back into the soil, fires ensure not only that species survive, but that they prosper.

Since the Lost Creek fire there has been plenty of such prosperity. Hiking routes throughout the Carbondale watershed – North Lost Creek, North Goat Creek and Upper Lynx Creek awash with fireweed and arnica – provide an opportunity to see a regenerating forest first-hand. Look for areas near the headwaters of Snowshoe Creek, where the fire was so hot it scorched tree roots and burned through the humus layer right down to rock. Extensive erosion has occurred. It may be decades before these forest areas are productive once again.

## The Castle's Great Green Secret: Vegetation and Diversity

The rejuvenation of the Castle after natural disturbances like the Lost Creek Fire and the 1995 flood is testimony to its ecological diversity and resiliency. Situated as it is, in the crosshairs of two weather systems but dominated by the plant-friendly Pacific Maritime climate, the Castle should be more known for its rich vegetation than it is. An estimated 824 vascular plants, over half the total species for all of Alberta, grow here. As well, a significant and still to be determined number of non-vascular mosses and lichens exist.

Beargrass along North Goat Creek the northernmost edge of its range in the Castle.

### Beargrass

Beargrass is one of the more celebrated plants that extends its northern limits into the Castle (mountain hollyhock, red and yellow monkey-flowers are some others). Beargrass is not really a grass but rather an evergreen herb of the Lily family. Neither does beargrass offer a meal for bears. The plant's clump of white flowers, which grow on a stalk up to six feet tall, is a treat for deer and elk. Beargrass lives a long time, producing long, thin leaves up to a metre tall, growing in dense tussocks. Beargrass is found on well-drained soils at elevations up to 2400 metres and is especially prominent in the West Castle Valley from the montane to the subalpine.

### Big Sagebrush

The southwest-facing slope of Whistler Mountain in the South Castle Valley boasts Alberta's largest stand of big sagebrush, a plant well known in the western U.S. This unique five-square-kilometre area is also home to at least 15 other provincially rare plants, including creeping mahonia, mariposa lily and snowbrush. Without proper protection, the big sagebrush area is continually threatened by motorized recreational use, random camping, equestrian use and cattle grazing.

Many of the plants here are rare, either unique to the Castle (there are 15 such species) or ones that grow here at the far edge of their natural range. Presently there are 132 provincially rare species of plants (38 of which are also nationally rare) growing in the Castle. Only Waterton has more rare plants. By comparison, Banff National Park has only 36 provincially rare plant species.

# Ecoregions

The Castle is made up of four ecoregions: foothills parkland, montane, subalpine and alpine. While the latter three ecoregions are the more dominant, the occurrence of foothills parkland makes the Castle, along with Waterton Lakes National Park, unique in Alberta. These are the only two places where at least four of the province's five ecoregions (only the boreal is missing) are found within their boundaries.

The idea of boundaries, particularly when it comes to establishing ecological areas, is a bit misleading to the average hiker. Rarely are natural boundaries clearly defined. Yet each ecoregion does have its own dominant physical characteristics and relationships with respect to precipitation, temperature, soils, plants and animals. In the Castle especially, with its dramatic rise in elevation over such short distances, these unique relationships can be witnessed more readily than in other areas along the Rocky Mountain Front. Moving east to west through the Castle you will likely cross all four ecoregions, beginning with the foothills parkland at the eastern edge of the Front Range canyons.

## Foothills Parkland

Foothills parkland, a ribbon of fescue grasses, aspen forest, spruce and willow running along the eastern edge of the foothills, from Calgary to Waterton Lakes National Park (where a significant portion is protected), has survived the best of all the parkland ecoregions. It has endured in some measure because its soil and climate, less favourable to crop farming, still support working ranches.

The Castle too supports relatively healthy foothills parkland. Sandwiched between the fescue ecoregion and the mixed forests of the montane and subalpine, foothills parkland crosses the tips of the Front Range valleys. Of these five drainages – Pincher Creek, North and South Drywood, Spionkop and Yarrow Creek – only the South Drywood is open for recreational vehicle use, a major contributor in damaging fescue grasses.

Before entering the subalpine one crosses a nice stretch of open montane in the Spionkop Valley.

## Ecozones, Ecoprovinces, Ecoregions

Canada is divided into 15 ecozones. At the top of the classification hierarchy, ecozones define Canada's ecological mosaic. Ecozones are large and generalized, each having more or less the same natural features, climate and organisms throughout. In the Castle two ecozones are represented: the Montane Cordillera and the Prairie. Still, as you might expect, there are many differences across these large landscapes. The more detailed differences are described at the ecoregion and ultimately ecodistrict levels. There are 194 ecoregions and 1,021 ecodistricts in Canada.

Hiking this transition zone between 1250 and 1500 metres, one characteristically passes through open meadows – a mix of oatgrass, rough fescue, June grass and bluebunch wheatgrass. Unlike cultivated grasses, these native fescues retain nutrients over the winter and are therefore crucial for elk, deer and moose. What distinguishes foothills parkland are the groves of trembling aspen typically found on upland slopes and the balsam poplar located in its moister sites. Common flowers and shrubs under the open aspen canopy include lupine, leafy aster, cow parsnip, stinging nettle, saskatoon and chokecherry. A distinctive feature of the foothills parkland aspen forest in the Castle is the wealth of glacier lily, which blooms in early to mid-May (later in higher elevations).

The warm, dry chinook winds and low precipitation so characteristic of the Front Range canyons make foothills parkland the hottest and driest of the four ecoregions, with a mean annual precipitation ranging from 500 to 650 millimetres. But it can get wet: in one 24-hour period from June 5 to 6, 1995, for example, 300 millimetres of rain was recorded at the Pincher Creek headwaters.

## Montane

The montane subregion boasts a large percentage of the ecological and biological diversity found within the Castle Carbondale watershed – a complex mosaic of forest and grassland that supports the majority of its plant and animal communities. Consequently, productive montane areas like those found in the Castle are valued for a number of often competing uses and activities: prime wildlife habitat, healthy watersheds, summer range for livestock, logging and recreation.

Despite being in such "high demand," the montane makes up less than 1 per cent of the province's landmass, most of it occurring along the southwest foothills. In the Banff/Bow Valley region, montane has suffered irreversibly from overdevelopment. In contrast, the Castle includes some of the largest remaining intact montane forests in the province.

Most of the Castle's montane is actually an extension of the ecoregion stretching south of the Chain Lakes. From the bordering ranchland to the north it encompasses much of the Castle's broad northeast section, as well as narrower sections within the Front Range, South Castle and West Castle River valleys between 1,000 and 1,900 metres in elevation.

Typically, montane is distinguished from the other ecoregions in the Castle by the presence of Douglas fir and limber pine – the fir on steep, south-facing slopes, the limber pine on exposed, extremely rocky outcrops. Limber pine normally associated with higher-elevation forests in the u.s. is found at the northern limit of its range here. Whistler Mountain is a place where conditions favour limber pine montane forest. Wildflowers and shrubs in the montane include blue clematis, beard tongue, fleabane, lupine, shrubby cinquefoil, wild rose, thimbleberry and bearberry.

However, with the Castle's wide range of environmental conditions, nothing here is written in stone. Closely connected to the foothills parkland, the montane too contains a significant mixture of rough fescue

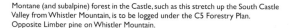

Montane (and subalpine) forest in the Castle, such as this stretch up the South Castle Valley from Whistler Mountain, is to be logged under the C5 Forestry Plan.
Opposite Limber pine on Whistler Mountain.

grasses on south- and west-facing slopes affected by sun, low rainfall and dry winds, especially in the Front Range valleys. Mid-elevation montane forests are often characterized by subalpine fir and Engelmann spruce, trees more suited to the subalpine, while, conversely, montane grasslands are found in the subalpine.

## Subalpine

The subalpine is the dominant ecoregion throughout the Rocky Mountain Cordillera and it constitutes over 30 per cent of the Castle's total area. Annual precipitation is higher here than any other Castle ecoregion, ranging from 460 millimetres annually in the drier Front Ranges to more than 1400 millimetres deep in the South Castle and West Castle valleys.

Before reaching the treeless alpine one typically passes through two subalpine zones. The lower subalpine (1650–1950 m) is primarily Engelmann spruce and subalpine fir forest, or lodgepole pine if recovering from a forest fire. In its typically moist, cool understorey, lichens, mosses and mushrooms can be found as well as false azalea, huckleberry, honeysuckle and alder. The subalpine understorey also contains a number of species that do not occur further north of the Castle in Alberta. These include not only the unique and much celebrated beargrass, but also thimbleberry, foam-flower and mountain boxwood.

Ascending through the upper subalpine (1950–2250 m), the forest becomes patchy and trees get smaller. Whitebark pine and subalpine larch, some of the oldest trees in the Canadian Rockies, are found in the upper elevations of the subalpine. The whitebark pine has been devastated over the years by white pine blister rust. Along the subalpine's uppermost elevations, wind and drier conditions result in distinctive twisted and stunted kruppelholz "crippled wood" spruce and pine stands.

Sometimes referred to as the "snow forest," dense tree cover in this ecoregion, especially in the lower subalpine, together with its cooler climate, makes snow accumulation an important component of the subalpine

The subalpine offers some of the most spectacular scenery in the Castle. Clockwise from top left: Middle Kootenay Pass; North Goat Creek; Upper Spionkop; Table Mountain.

ecology. Wildflowers benefit from this extra wetness, especially when it overlaps with the radiant early-summer sun. Avalanche slopes and their successional vegetation communities are also dominant features of this ecoregion.

The presence of subalpine fir at lower elevations, normally associated with montane forest, is an unusual feature of the Castle region. Equally unusual are the montane grasses to be found in the subalpine (and alpine meadows), especially on steep southerly and westerly aspects in the Front Range. The trails accessing high ridges and passes of the Continental Divide such as Three Lakes Ridge and North Kootenay Pass also offer excellent routes through the subalpine into the alpine.

## Alpine

The alpine extends above the treeline on exposed, rocky slopes (typically above 2200 metres in the Castle). It is easily the coldest ecoregion, with a mean temperature of around 6°c from May through September and substantially colder in the winter months. Mean annual precipitation ranges from 420 to 850 millimetres, although it rains most along the Continental Divide. In this cold, harsh environment, treeline

### Larch

One of the pleasures of fall in the Castle is exploring larch stands in the subalpine. From mid-September until early October larch are easy to spot, their needles golden against a backdrop of grey, snow-dusted rock. There are numerous good hikes where you can see larch. A nice stand awaits hikers heading to the saddle at the end of South Drywood Creek. The back side of Barnaby Ridge above the lower South Fork lake is also a favourite of local hikers.

Fringed grass-of-parnassus.

elevation varies depending on local factors such as slope aspect, wind exposure, the depth of the snow and how late it melts. Much of the alpine has little or no soil. Where soil does exist it is generally thin, collected by the wind and deposited in cracks among exposed rocks.

But this does not mean the alpine is devoid of plants and animals. The high elevations in the Castle offer plenty of plants surviving at their limits. Vegetation tends to be small – an adaptation to having virtually no frost-free days. In moist, protected meadows where snow lingers, sedges, including black alpine sedge, bluebells and anemones are common. In the drier, exposed areas brilliant wildflowers bloom, such as alpine forget-me-not, paintbrush, harebell and penstemon. Plants seeking protection between the exposed rocks and boulders include moss campion, mountain avens, pussytoes and saxifrage. In the most exposed areas lichens take over.

While mountain heathers abound in more northern latitudes, they are noticeably rare here. On the other hand, beargrass occurs above its normal range in the low alpine meadows, a unique feature of the Castle.

Many animals range regularly between the subalpine and alpine subregions, including Columbian ground squirrel, pika, hoary marmot, grizzly bear, mountain goat and bighorn sheep. White-tailed ptarmigan, rock wrens, gray-crowned rosy finch and water pipit are some of the alpine bird species.

## Has It Given Enough? Threats Facing the Castle

*One cannot describe the living attributes of the Castle without confronting that which threatens them.*

— Journal entry, August 2005

Arguably the largest threat to the Castle today – to its watersheds, its vegetation and wildlife – is an intensive 20-year logging plan for the southern Eastern Slopes. Drafted in 2005 by the provincial Sustainable Resource Development ministry, the C5 Forest Management Plan sets a course to log Crown forest from Longview to the Waterton Lakes National Park boundary, including the remaining old growth in the upper South and West Castle Valleys. It's an old story the Castle has been forced to endure time and time again.

Commercial logging in the Castle can be traced back to the late 1880s, when sawmills provided logs and lumber for railway construction and human settlement. Timber extraction steadily increased as mining and settlement placed additional demands on local tree species, especially Douglas fir. To accommodate the boom, timber berths were issued directly to companies such as the Canadian Pacific Railway. These exclusive permits allowed relatively unregulated logging, especially in the Crowsnest corridor, and remained in effect until the mid-1960s,

Clockwise top left: alpine arnica below Mount Coulthard; penstemon; mountain buttercup; paintbrush.

Timber at the turn of the century and into the Depression years was primarily used locally to build houses, barns and light industry. Here two horse teams haul timber out of the eastern edge of the Castle, west of Twin Butte. Photo by Bert Riggall courtesy of the Kootenai Brown Pioneer Village and Pincher Creek Historical Society.
Opposite: A logged Douglas fir in a basin below Rainy Ridge: in the footsteps of ancient giants.

when new licences and quotas replaced them. With a new provincial quota system in place operators both large and small continued to log in earnest.

If the land seemed inexhaustible, wood was not. Clean, dependable water was also threatened. Amid the din of chainsaws and falling timber, naturalists were beginning to understand that forests store water and release it slowly. They recognized that the continuing destruction of forests threatened the water supply the region's growing population would need. But timber and cattle were the commodities that drove the Alberta economy of the early 20th century. Like the oil and gas that followed, logging has proven to be a difficult industry to rein in.

The 1980s also bore witness to salvage logging of lodgepole pine stands infested by the mountain pine beetle. This insect is naturally kept in check by wildfires and long periods of extremely cold weather, but bolstered by a string of warmer winters, especially in the British Columbia Interior, the beetle has once again begun to infest forests in and around the Castle. The return of the mountain pine beetle has helped frame the Alberta government's plan to log the Eastern Slopes.

Quickly denounced by environmental groups as well as local landowners, the C5 Forest Management Plan was set out for public review, where it found further opposition. In spring 2007 the Minister for Sustainable Resource Development decided to postpone the plan pending further review. According to some in the environmental community, such as Nigel Douglas of the Alberta Wilderness Association (AWA), the postponement was "an encouraging sign that maybe the Alberta government is beginning to recognize that Alberta's forests are more than just vertical timber." Still, the government's 60-year track record of environmental non-protection stands as a sober reminder.

Rather than wait for a government that will in all likelihood endorse its own plan, the AWA, the Sierra Club of Canada, the Castle-Crown Wilderness Coalition and the Canadian Parks & Wilderness Society, among others, have put forward their own plan to designate the Castle a

combination provincial and wildlands park. Within the Andy Russell–I'tai sah kòp Park as it is being proposed, 90 per cent of the Castle would fall under wildlands designation and would be off limits for industrial use. The remaining 10 per cent that corresponds to the lower Castle River valley would constitute the provincial park, including the existing campgrounds, staging areas, organization camps and major public roads.

The compelling argument for a park is to establish protection for the Castle under the Provincial Parks Act and discontinue the current multiple-use-area conservation strategy, which has failed so badly in all its various manifestations throughout decades. Presently the only area with protected status in the Castle is a small, 232-acre reserve located immediately downstream from the Castle Mountain Resort. This West Castle Wetland Ecological Reserve was established in 1998 to protect wetland habitat for beaver, spawning trout and amphibians. Oddly, neither the Alberta Forest Service nor Fish & Wildlife, both of which are part of the Sustainable Resource Development ministry, have the authority to establish such protected areas, even for safeguarding critical wildlife habitat. Instead, the responsibility falls to

## Old Growth

Historically the forests of the Castle were likely one-third old growth characterized by Engelmann spruce and subalpine fir as well as, in the South and West Castle valleys, whitebark pine some hundreds of years old. At lower elevations aspen and lodgepole pine can be found mixed with the spruce, and also Douglas fir.

With plenty of decomposing logs and standing dead trees, along with a mixture of ground vegetation and nutrient-rich soils, old-growth forests support a large variety of plants and animals. Species such as the Canada lynx, marten and interior bird species can survive nowhere other than in the interior of large patches of old-growth forest. Fallen logs provide dens for hibernating bears, homes for red-back voles and marten and stream debris for fish habitat.

Since the 1930s approximately 50 per cent of the old-growth forest cover in the Castle has been lost to logging. While the logging industry typically regards old-growth forests as "decadent stands," advocates of sustainable forestry recommend that 25 per cent of forests be old growth at any one time. Today only 10 per cent of the Castle's forests are considered old growth.

Tourism, Parks, Recreation & Culture. To date, the provincial government has resisted the creation of any park in the Castle, preferring "to keep the forest open for multiple uses."

## Protection

*Anticipating and directing the means whereby human beings transform nature are belief systems as well as science.*

— Stephen Most

Travelling through the Crown of the Continent from all directions, from Pine Ridge along Highway 6, from the open grass slopes of the MX Ranch above Pincher Creek, through the time warp of the Crowsnest Pass, one feels enveloped in a classic Western landscape where little seems to have changed. Contributing to the illusion is a population density that hovers around 10 people per square mile (compared to the North American average of 70) and where the populations of the core communities are still less than 5,000 inhabitants. The Rocky Mountain spine, *Mo'kakiikin*, the Crown, the Castle remain by and large rural landscapes.

Step out into a broader landscape, however, and a different picture emerges. Beyond the Crown's theoretical boundaries, but less than a three-hour drive from the Castle, sits Calgary, its rapidly expanding population now topping one million. Pressure from outside to subdivide ranchland, to create residential and commercial real estate from agricultural land, has been present ever since the first timber and mining leases came into existence, and today, Alberta's largest city, with its ceaseless need for resources, dominates the West's political and economic mood like never before. The closest large u.s. city to the Crown is Spokane, population 250,000. But though it is one of the fastest growing cities in the Rockies, it still lies two States away, and any impact it may have on the mountain region pales in comparison with Calgary's. Clearly it would appear that protection of wild open spaces needs to come from the Canadian side.

133

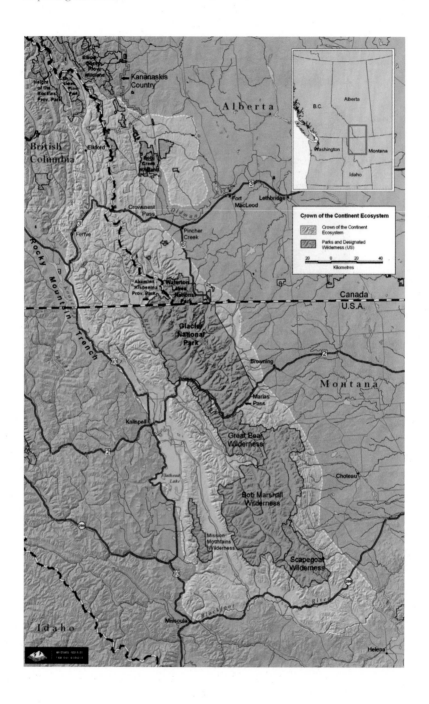

Such is not the case, however. When looking at a modern map of the Crown of the Continent one is immediately struck, besides the scarcity of towns, by the full and balanced deck of land types and land uses on both sides of the international border: mountains, forests, rivers and lakes, ranchland and farmland, dams, roads and railways. Pull the parks and designated wilderness area cards out of the deck, however, and the map changes dramatically. Wilderness protection in the Crown of the Continent is disproportionately skewed to south of the border. From the u.s. border to the southern tip of the Crown of the Continent almost three million acres of public land is either designated wilderness or protected as a park, with the Bob Marshall Wilderness and Glacier National Park each accounting for one million acres.[12]

On the Canadian side, despite the acknowledged pressure for land and resources in southern Alberta, the numbers pale significantly. Barely 625,000 acres within the Crown of the Continent (less than a quarter of the u.s. total) have some form of designated wilderness protection. Of this total the two largest areas – Waterton Lakes National Park and the Elbow-Sheep Wildlands Park – are each less than 200,000 acres. The rest is made up of a hodgepodge of minor provincial parks, natural areas, heritage rangelands and ecological reserves such as the small West Castle Wetland Ecological Reserve.

This discrepancy should not be unexpected: the u.s. has a longer history of selecting and designating protected areas than Canada does. (The first national park in the world was Yellowstone, authorized in 1872. Canada's first, Banff, was designated in 1885.) The conservation movement in the u.s. is well established, and with a list of successful wilderness designations it can toast the names of John Muir, Edward Sargent and later Aldo

Human Landmarks in the Crown of the Continent Ecosystem. Map created by the Miistakis Institute. First published in *Crown of the Continent: Profile of a Treasured Landscape,* 2002. Below the 49th parallel there is four times as much protected area within the Crown of the Continent as there is on the Canadian side. The Castle, just north of Waterton Lakes National Park, remains unprotected.

12    The largest roadless expanse in the u.s. Rocky Mountains lies within the 1.5 million acres of connected mountain and forest made up of the Bob Marshall, Scapegoat and Great Bear Wilderness areas. There are no roads across the mountains between u.s. Route 2 in the north and Montana Route 200 in the south, a straight-line distance of more than 160 km (100 miles).

Leopold and Bob Marshall as its champions. In 1935 Leopold and Marshall, foresters turned conservationists, helped found the Wilderness Society, which later spearheaded an eight-year campaign that culminated in the most important piece of wilderness legislation in North America to date, the Wilderness Act of 1964.[13]

The significance of the modern conservation movement cannot be overstated when it comes to protecting wilderness. Most successes in nature conservation can be attributed to the movement's own efforts. Dave Foreman, in his influential book *Rewilding North America: A Vision for Conservation in the 21st Century*, writes passionately about the role and philosophy of the founders of the movement, particularly those of Leopold and his land ethic, when establishing his own vision for a network of contiguous protected areas along the Rocky Mountain spine into Canada.

Overlooked or underestimated by many conservationists, including Foreman, much of Leopold's vision of a restored natural landscape depended on the efforts of private landowners. With public lands already being compromised and the politics too contentious, Leopold felt private land was where the greatest success in preserving nature lay. He also called on individuals to seek their own personal ethical relationship with the land, a relationship that depended on contact and direct accountability.

Just as Canadian settlement patterns paralleled settlement south of the border, so has u.s. conservation history largely informed the conservation and environmental movement to the north. It is not without irony that just at the time the modern conservation movement and national park systems were being launched, North American Indians, including the Siksika, Kainai, Piikani and Ktunaxa, were being removed from their traditional lands. Protected status through a national park and wilderness system largely informed by conservation biology and modern ecology has often come at the expense of previous tenants and with disregard

---

13      The Wilderness Act of 1964 created the legal definition of wilderness in the United States: " ... an area where the earth and its community of life are untrammeled by man, where man himself is a visitor who does not remain." With the stroke of his pen President Lyndon B. Johnson immediately protected nine million acres (36,000 km²) of federal land. Today the National Wilderness Preservation System in the United States covers more than 106 million acres (429,000 km²).

Clockwise from top left: random camping "village" in Lynx Recreational Camping Area; logging for ski hill expansion on Haig Ridge; abandoned random camping fire pit along West Castle River; vegetation damage from vehicles on South Kootenay trail; illegal trail in the alpine of North Kootenay Pass.
If we are facing a wilderness crisis, it is not because of how ecosystems function, but rather because of how our ethical systems dysfunction.

for indigenous land use practices and sacred sites. After all, wilderness designation is really only land use designation with a nobler title.

This is not to say modern environmental science supporting a vision of wilderness is not to be used as a foundation for rewilding places like the Castle. That would be foolish. But while science can accurately describe the crisis wilderness is facing – habitat loss, species extinction, climate change … – it cannot wholly explain why this crisis is happening. Science cannot explain why people continue to drive their vehicles into restricted zones and damage fragile vegetation. It cannot explain why some people persist in poaching, or why they build fires during fire bans, or why developers continue to expand ski hills and industrialists continue to disregard conservation in favour of further detrimental development. If we are facing a wilderness conservation, protection and restoration crisis, it is not because of how ecosystems function, but rather because of how our ethical systems dysfunction.[14]

---

14       Adapted from Donald Worster's *The Wealth of Nature*.

# The Trail Ahead

*Restoration and reclamation are distinct terms. Restoration involves returning an area to its pre-disturbance, natural state. Reclamation means returning a site (usually an industrial site) to some productive use following disturbance, but not necessarily to a natural state.*

— "Bringing it Back: A Restoration Framework
for the Castle Wilderness"

*"If wind has shaped the soil profile of the prairie, if bison have influenced vegetation, if prairie dogs have dug holes all over the place, then humans have been active, too."*

— Donald Worster

Somewhere in the midst of my summer of hiking the Castle, between my early near-bear experience up Three Lakes Ridge and the black bear sow that my wife, Emily, encountered as we descended Table Mountain in late August, I began to wonder what stories would be told in the decades and generations to follow. Would someone be able to tell a story like Emily's about their first sighting of a bear in the wild? Or would the future transformation of this area be so profound, its shift so abrupt, that either there are no bears left or no one is able (or worse, not willing) to witness wild places, when all that's left are tired, worn-out accounts of no consequence. I find it strange that I thought less about what this landscape might *look* like and more about the stories being told.

William Kittredge in *Who Owns the West?* writes that the stories we construct and uncover are imaginary maps "in which we see our purposes defined," and when the world that surrounds us "drifts" as it inevitably does, "we have to reinvent our understandings and our reasons for doing things." In a changing world, old "maps" don't work anymore.

Reimagining a landscape or reinventing reasons for doing things is often resisted, even resented. We ignore the changing landscape, sticking to the stories that sanction what we already know, reconfirming how little we want to know. When others tell us to rethink points of view or test assumptions, we get testy.

When I mention to someone that motorized vehicles today are destroying the Castle and should be banned, and they reply that the Castle has "always been this way," what exactly are they saying? "Always"? What "way"?

And when conservation biologist Reed Noss states[15] that "the model natural ecosystem complex is the presettlement vegetation and associated abiotic elements," what does he mean? Which snapshot, which presettlement is he referring to?

I like the idea of maps as stories. It acknowledges right up front that we cannot go back, but it nonetheless puts the power of stories and the consequences for tomorrow in our hands today. But it is not the easiest of notions. First there are still stories untold that should be heard, not as a way to live in the past but as a way to acquire knowledge and perspective with which to plan for the future. Unfortunately we could not survive using Ac ko Mok ki's map, yet we still need Ac ko Mok ki's story. Without his story how would we notice that the world has drifted and that the maps we're using are simply getting us lost? Isn't it in part because stories like Ac ko Mok ki's have been buried that a place like the Castle is so

Fallen larch needles on rocks below Windsor Ridge.

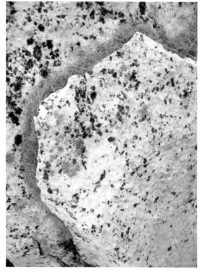

---

15      As quoted in Flores 2001.

detached from the broader landscape that many just disregard it, log it and litter it with slash, trash and noise; or conversely that in our hope for a wilder place, the Castle becomes a romanticized landscape and a stage for legal wrangling and endless policy mood swings?

# An Invitation to Hike the Castle

*The closer you get to real matter, rock air fire wood, boy, the more spiritual the world is.*

— Gary Snyder (as the character Japhy Ryder
in Jack Kerouac's novel *The Dharma Bums*)

Gary Snyder, to many the poet laureate of wild places, is speaking to his "footsore" and reprobate companion Ray Smith (Jack Kerouac) as they hike up Mount Tamalpais, a readily accessed 2,600-foot peak across the Golden Gate bridge from San Francisco. The year is 1956. Both are undoubtedly unaware that not even a hundred years have passed since Blakiston laboured over windfall-littered indigenous trails through the Castle to cross the Continental Divide, the mythical barrier to the Pacific Coast. Snyder, an able mountaineer himself, was more than likely aware of the fact that in 1857 (while Blakiston and others on the Palliser Expedition were claiming territory for the Dominion) a group of mountaineers back in England had formed the Alpine Club, opening the door for the proliferation of hiking clubs and organizations across the Empire. Hiking had become an activity of leisure and was seen as the ideal way of being in the world "out of doors, relying on one's own feet, neither producing nor destroying," as Rebecca Solnit puts it.

Of course, one's own feet can produce irreparable damage. We constantly forget that other creatures, five kingdoms worth, also live in the Castle. A misplaced step can destroy a pincushion of moss campion that has flourished for 350 years. A trail of human garbage can "socialize" a grizzly and quickly destroy its free-roaming spirit. A well-intentioned ford of a creek can destroy vital redds of threatened bull trout. To protect the Castle, therefore, one must hike with a renewed commitment to preserve what remains and restore what has been damaged. And whether we tell them beyond our circle of friends and acquaintances or not, the stories of our experiences need to be told.

For Snyder the ritual of a hike is more than mere experience and goes deeper than "a way of being …" In the spirit of the backbone of the world it is the practice of accessing that which is one and the same, both mind and matter. Destroy one and the other ceases. Seen in this way, hiking is salvation. It is also for Snyder a political, social and spiritual revolutionary act. "A hike is not a quest, it does not attain a goal, it goes round and round, on and on," writes Rebecca Solnit.

In this century, when the natural world is dying all around us, when according to Gary Paul Nabhan the earth is losing species at an unprecedented rate of one every 20 minutes, it is important to see the Castle as a landscape of hope rather than a final stand against the impending tide. Despite the onslaught of modernization, the Castle, though battered and torn, can still inspire us.

We have names for all the goat feed
Campion, lichen, sorrel
We have taxonomy, geology, the camera
and the transit – we have everything
in the world to know
this mountain

Yet look back now
and see it change into a waterfall
a pillar of salt
a tower of smoke

It's time to write a different text
for all that we have captured
is this tuft of fine, white hair

— Sid Marty, "On Lineham Ledge,"
in *Sky Humour*

# The Trail
# Guide

For those more familiar with the "hiking highways" of Banff, Jasper and Kananaskis, the Castle is a unique experience. First, the Castle is not a park, national or provincial, at least not yet. Routes follow established pack trails, game trails and logging and resource exploration roads, and thus you will find no formal trail maintenance, no information services and no facilities. Although a network of numbered trail signs for ATVs and snowmobiles does exist (there may also be an occasional piece of flagging tape or a cairn marking a route) they offer only marginal help for the hiker. Even with the Alberta government's motorized-vehicle trail map, the mixed bag of illegal ATV tracks and old roads can lead the unsuspecting hiker off the preferred route.

# How to Use this Guide

The guide is divided into four areas: Front Range Valleys, South Castle Valley, West Castle Valley and Carbondale-Lynx. Although the routes described are some of the most popular and rewarding, this book does not describe all the hikes one might take in the Castle. With topographic maps, compass or GPS and strong route-finding skills the hardy hiker can find numerous other short jaunts, scrambles, loops and epic expeditions. Trails are normally self-evident, but sections on some can become overgrown or washed out, depending on recent weather or lack of use.

### Descriptions

The trail descriptions, times and distances are written for hikers. On some routes a mountain bike may be suggested to help get you to the trailhead quicker than having to experience a dusty slog along a logging or well site road. For the most part I have tried to keep overt opinions in check – not always an easy task. But one thing is certain: right and left in the route descriptions apply to the direction of travel.

## Difficulty Rating

The difficulty rating for this guide is fairly generous, favouring the more novice to intermediate hiker who may be unacquainted with the area. Other than that there is no easy way to classify a trail. What is easy for one person is difficult for another. Hiking, regardless of the ease of terrain, has inherent hazards; certain skills and fitness are required. Pay attention to route descriptions. Read ahead to determine your choices, and if the going gets too tough, turn back and try an easier trail.

## Hiking Times

Everyone hikes at a different rate. Some push hard, head down, straight to the summit; others literally stop to smell the wild roses along the way. Weather too can affect hiking times considerably, as can the condition of the trail, elevation gain and further exploration along the way. A normal hiking rate is 4 km/h. Use this figure only as a general guide.

## Maps

The maps in this book should not replace topographic maps. Instead they serve as a snapshot of the route you are about to take. It is strongly recommended that you purchase the 1:50,000 NATIONAL TOPOGRAPHIC SYSTEM maps for the area: Sage Creek 82G/1, Beaver Mines 82G/8, Flathead 82G/7, Blairmore 82G/9 and Crowsnest 82G/10. Also, the Adventure Guide and Topographic Map of Southern Alberta, published by the Southwest Alberta Business Development Centre, is useful though not detailed enough for route finding. The Alberta Sustainable Resources Development ministry's winter and summer trail map basically tells you where motorized vehicles should and should not be.

Because of natural changes in the area, the actual sections of a trail marked on all maps can be outdated. This book endeavours to compensate for these discrepancies.

**Considerations**

- When hiking above treeline, use existing trails or walk on rocks and snow where possible to avoid damaging fragile vegetation.
- No registration is required for day hiking or overnight backpack trips. Still, let someone know your expected route and return time.
- While dogs are not required to wear a leash, owners should be able to control them at all times.
- An Alberta fishing licence is required.
- Leave no trace and pack out your garbage – perishables and non-perishables alike.
- Clean up your campsite.
- Obey fire bans and restrictions. Check with Forestry for the current fire hazard rating.

# Hazards and Concerns

### Weather

Hiking season generally starts around mid-April and runs until early November. Naturally, the main obstacle early and late in the season is snow, and snow can fall during any month. This *is* Rocky Mountain country after all. On the other hand, summer temperatures can rise above 30°c and in the subalpine and alpine, where shade and water can be at a premium, heatstroke and dehydration can be a concern. Also, clouds and thunderstorms brought on by late afternoon heating accompanied by lightning can leave hikers unexpectedly exposed. If you see threatening late afternoon clouds rolling in, climb down from open ridges.

### River Crossings

The Castle (South and West branches), the Carbondale and Lynx Creek can be impassable during a particularly high spring runoff. Other creeks and tributaries coming off the mountains can also be treacherous and numbingly cold early in the hiking season. While a few bridges exist in the Castle, expect to get wet. See the route descriptions for information on crossing waterways.

## Loose Rock

As mentioned in the geology section, much of the rock in the Castle is ancient sedimentary rubble. Be aware any time you find yourself hiking through a steep gully. If the route permits, stay some distance away from steep rock faces, Use sheep trails wherever possible when scrambling along scree slopes.

## Bears

Bear attacks are infrequent in the Castle and seeing a bear in the wild is an exhilarating experience like few others. So it is with mixed feelings that I include bears in the hazard section. Always be aware of the possibility of a bear encounter, particularly in spring and in late summer coming into fall when the animals are focused on protecting their cubs and food. The best prevention is to deny them access to food and garbage. Your best defence is constant awareness, especially when travelling through thick willows, near streams or in windy weather, as vegetation and ambient noise may mask your approach. Bear spray and other deterrents do not replace the need to be vigilant.

## Ticks etc.

From early spring to mid-June ticks can be a problem, especially if you find yourself in mountain sheep terrain. Wear light-coloured clothing so they can be more readily seen, and check yourself after each hike. The verdict is still out on the presence of Lyme disease in the area, but better to take precautions than risks.

Mosquitos can be a nuisance, especially in the valley bottoms and when it has been a particularly wet spring. Typically the ridges where the winds blow offer a refuge. I've seen whitetail deer sitting up in the subalpine breeze trying to get away from the bugs.

## Hunters

Between September and November an estimated 4,387 hunters, upwards of 275 per day, visit the Castle. Sunday is considered a No Hunting day, but don't take this for granted. During hunting season always wear brightly coloured clothing. Also be warned that inconsiderate hunters may dress out a kill along or near the trail and leave the offal behind, which may attract bears. Hunters can also be the source of valuable information regarding bear sightings and routes, however.

Elk and deer seem to know when hunting season is upon them and they become hard to spot. They either move out of the Castle onto private land or stay well hidden and skittish.

## Motorized Vehicles

Unfortunately, ATV and motorcycles can spoil a good day of hiking – hours of clean air, stillness and solitude rudely interrupted. Thankfully, most riders keep their speed down and are respectful of hikers on the trail. Best to step off to the side and let them and their exhaust pass.

## Horses

Most horses used in the backcountry are sure-footed and calm, or at least for the riders' sake they should be. When meeting up with a group of riders, move to the up-slope side of the trail, stay visible and stay still until they pass.

# Hiking Tips/What to Pack

Because weather can change suddenly and a mountain hike is not a simple walk in the park, what you wear and what you pack, even if it is only a daypack, should include a few essentials and the odd luxury besides your lunch ...

- A sturdy, comfortable pair of hiking boots (and an extra pair of dry socks)
- A water repellent windbreaker
- One warm layer, whether it's a fleece jacket, vest or wool sweater
- A long-sleeved shirt
- Insect repellent
- Sunscreen
- Plenty of drinking water – a 2- to 3-litre water bladder is a good purchase
- If camping overnight, some form of water purification to prevent *Giardia* infection
- Map(s), compass (if you know how to use one), GPS (if you can afford one)
- Binoculars
- Pair of sturdy sandals for crossing rivers and creeks

# Trails+
# Routes

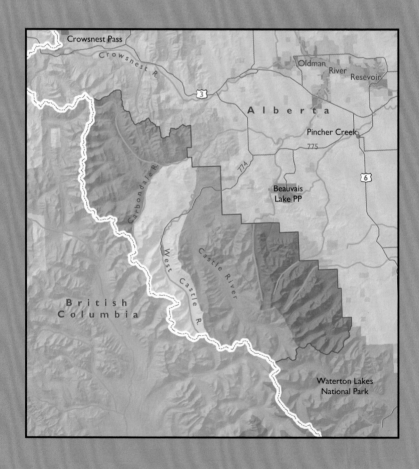

Crowsnest Pass

Crowsnest R.

Oldman River Resevoir

**3**

**A l b e r t a**

Pincher Creek

775

774

**6**

Carbondale R.

Beauvais Lake PP

West Castle R.

Castle River

**B r i t i s h
C o l u m b i a**

Waterton Lakes National Park

The Carbondale area is the northern portion of the Castle and is closest to the Crowsnest Pass. The trails – predominantly old logging roads – access some of the tallest peaks and most rugged terrain in the Castle.

The South Castle Valley and West Castle Valley receive unusually high precipitation and are important contributors to the Oldman River Basin. Many small streams drain the upper side valleys, their flows regulated by forest cover and the storage capacity of spongy old-growth soils and numerous alpine and subalpine wetlands, including numerous high-elevation lakes. These watersheds offer tremendous remote backcountry experiences in their headwaters, and seasonal whitewater paddling in their lower reaches.

The Front Range watersheds on the east side of the Castle are unique in Canada. These canyons, mountains and ridges come straight out of the rolling grasslands, and the views east from their summits go on forever. Here one can walk through four ecological regions – from foothills parkland grasslands and aspen groves, up through montane and subalpine forests and crest an alpine meadow – all within a distance of less than four kilometres. The area is dry and water can be scarce once above the valley floors.

# Upper Carbondale Drainage

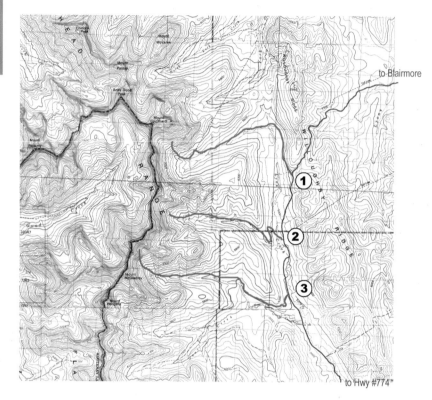

## I. UPPER LYNX CREEK

| | |
|---|---|
| Distance: | 6.3 km to cave in SE wall of Mt. Coulthard |
| Time: | 2+ hrs. to head of valley, 3 hrs. to cave |
| Rating: | moderate |
| Start elevation: | 1730 m |
| Low elevation | 1633 m |
| End elevation: | 1973 m |
| Max. elevation gain: | 340 m |
| Mode of travel: | bike and/or hike, scramble |
| Terrain: | dirt road, double track, dry creek bed, bush, open alpine meadow |
| Maps: | 82G/10 Crowsnest |
| Note: | CAMP Trail #39 is a popular ATV route, part of a network of trails between Lynx Creek and South York Creek. |

**Overview and Comments**

This is a moderate but relatively short trail into the steep, south cirque of Mount Coulthard. Like other trails in the Lynx/Goat drainages, the first couple of kilometres follow dirt road through open meadow and burned forest. Some route finding through thick vegetation near the head of the valley is necessary before entering the cirque. The more adventuresome can explore the cliffs and ledges above on Coulthard. A payoff is the cooling water that falls over a prominent overhang on Mount Coulthard's south face.

Mount McLaren, Mount Parrish, Andy Good Peak and Coulthard form one of the largest massifs in the region. Mount Coulthard is also known for its major cave system.

## Access

*from Crowsnest Pass:*
Drive south on the Lynx (Sartoris) Road from Blairmore for 10 km. Approximately 1 km after crossing a cattle guard at the top of Willoughby Ridge, look for a road heading sharply to the right. Turn down this road and park to the side.

*from Beaver Mines:*
Drive south on Highway 774 for 13 km and take the Castle recreation road west (just before the Castle River bridge). Turn left at the T junction to the Lynx Creek Road (11.4 km) and follow the Lynx Creek Road for 12 km. After crossing a bridge, drive another 2.5 km and look for a road heading left. Turn down this road and park to the side.

## Route Description

There is nothing special for the first 2 km, a steady descent to the valley bottom. After 1.4 km CAMP Trail #40 intersects the road. Stay straight. Continue as the trail bends left and crosses Lynx Creek. After crossing, begin a gradual ascent to a bench above the creek. Stay straight as another signed trail (#41) forks right. Heavy use of ATVs has made the area boggy.

Mount Coulthard looms ahead; paintbrush alongside the trail.

The next 1.5 km stay fairly straight through open meadow and old burn, with views ahead to Mount Coulthard. Spring-fed bogs and puddles make the trail muddy in spots. Pass through a short section of forest that escaped burning when the crown fire jumped the valley, missing the smaller trees. After 250 m, cross Lynx Creek. Continue for a short distance and then cross Lynx Creek again.

Back on the north side of the creek, continue through another burned forest stand, detouring around a washed-out section before picking up trail alongside a mossy spring. Past this section the trail begins its gradual ascent to the head of the valley. Entering an older spruce/fir forest, come to where the trail makes a hard right. An older trail continues straight ahead but dead-ends quickly. Instead, take the right turn and continue up a steeper ascent through forest cover, arriving at an obvious cutline heading north.

The trail heading north accesses the south fork of York Creek. An ATV double track looks like it might be a direct route to the cirque. Instead, this illegal trail ends in a clearing of cow parsnip, fireweed, blowdown and old stumps. To get to the headwaters of Lynx Creek and the cirque, follow the overgrown cutline south down to Lynx Creek.

After negotiating 250 m of blowdown and knee-high vegetation, turn upstream and follow the gravel creek bed as it swings back to the north. After 100 m following the creek, bushwack on an angle up the fairly

View out from under cliff overhang on Mount Coulthard.

steep north bank until the terrain begins to level off. From here you can either continue up the creek into the main cirque or head up a secondary drainage and major avalanche slope leading to what looks like a cave but is actually an overhanging cliff and cascade.

To get to the cliff, climb up the steep slope below toward a prominent cliff band on the south face of Coulthard. In late summer when the cascade is not much more than a steady trickle, stand under the overhang and let the water cool you off.

### Mount Coulthard

2642 m (8668 ft.)

Located on the Continental Divide at the headwaters of Andy Good Creek and North York Creek, the mountain was named after R.W. Coulthard, a prominent geologist and mining engineer in the late 1800s. He became general manager of West Canadian Coal Co. in the early part of the 20th century.

## 2. SNOWSHOE CREEK

| | |
|---|---|
| Distance: | 5 km to subalpine meadow |
| Total time: | 2.5+ hrs. to head of valley; 3.0 to base of Mt. McGladrey |
| Rating: | moderate |
| Start elevation: | 1541 m |
| End elevation: | 1812 m |
| Max. elevation gain: | 281 m |
| Mode of travel: | bike and/or hike, scramble |
| Maps: | 82G/10 Crowsnest |
| Terrain: | dirt road, double track, dry creek bed, bush, open alpine meadow |
| Note: | Because of its relatively short length and deadfall, this is not much used by ATVs. |

### Overview and Comments

This is a relatively short, moderately easy trail to the bowl to the north of Mount McGladrey. Like other trails in the Lynx/Goat drainages, the first 2 km are straightforward dirt double track through open, burned spruce/fir with some boggy sections. Although the thick vegetation near the end makes some route finding necessary, the trail is well worth the effort to see the natural reclamation after the Lost Creek fire.

This is also a good hike to see where the Lost Creek fire not only torched forest crown but also extensively burned surface and subsurface organic matter, scarifying and sterilizing topsoil and leaving exposed, burned roots and bedrock.

## Access

*from Crowsnest Pass:*
Drive south on the Lynx (Sartoris) Road from Blairmore crossing cattle guard at the top of Willoughby ridge before dropping to Lynx Creek. Approximtely 500 m before crossing bridge over Lynx Creek there is a pull-off accessing a logging road trail.

*from Beaver Mines:*
Drive south on Highway 774 for 13 km and take the Castle recreation road west (just before the Castle River bridge). Turn left at the T junction onto the Lynx Creek Road (11.4 km) and follow the road for 12 km. After crossing a bridge look for a pull-off on west side of the road accessing a logging road.

## Route Description

The trail starts out as dirt road, but the double track quickly splits after 400 m. Take the left fork, what amounts to a sweeping s turn, gradually ascending over the next few kilometres through burned lodgepole pine/spruce forest. Later in the summer the understorey is awash with fireweed.

Now up on the bench the road heads northwest up a very gradual incline. Views from the meadows are open, with Pengelly and McGladrey clearly visible at the head of the valley. The trail continues straight through a mix of burn and open forest. After 2 km of easy going, a series of springs make the trail wet and boggy (3.5 km).

Less than 1 km later the double track crosses a side creek. On the opposite bank a No ATVs sign is posted. The trail from this point is very

Clockwise from top left: Open bench with panorama of McGladrey; end of ATV access (4 km); in some places the fire left the valley floor unscathed; new growth in the burn; upper reaches of Snowshoe Creek.
Opposite: Severely burned understorey at head of valley.

hard to distinguish and difficult to negotiate because of thick vegetation and dead snags. Instead, make your way left down a short distance to Snowshoe Creek and follow the creek upstream. By mid-summer the creek has gone underground this far up the valley, so travelling is relatively easy.

After 500 m, the creek bed opens to subalpine meadow. The burned forest up from the north bank and up onto the shoulder is well worth exploring to see the effects of the Lost Creek fire. By mid-July the arnica set off against the blackened standing dead trees is brilliant. It is also interesting to see the effects of erosion owing to the extensive loss of subsoil organic matter.

## 3. NORTH GOAT CREEK

| | |
|---|---|
| Distance: | 6.5 km to base of Mt. McGladrey |
| Time: | 2.5+ hrs. to head of valley; 3.0 hrs. to base of McGladrey |
| Rating: | moderate |
| Start elevation: | 1512 m |
| End elevation: | 2163 m |
| Max. elevation gain: | 652 m |
| Mode of travel: | bike and/or hike, scramble |
| Maps: | 82G/10 Crowsnest |
| Terrain: | dirt road, double track, game trails, open alpine meadow |
| Note: | 4WD users on early sections. |

**Overview and Comments**

This is a moderately easy trail, a gentle rolling double track that accesses the base of Mount McGladrey and Mount Pengelly. Goat Creek drainage has been logged extensively and clear cuts dominate the lower slopes. Fire in 2003 scorched much of what remained. The first 2.8 km are easy and relatively uneventful.

Dirt road passes through open, logged and burned lodgepole forest. Once through the old logged meadow the double track road/trail takes on the characteristics of other east Clark Range drainages – patchy spruce and fir forest, thick alder shrub and fire succession undergrowth. What makes this hike/bike truly worthwhile are the stunning slopes below McGladrey and Pengelly: their sharp-thrusted limestone/karst formations, steep rockwalls and striking peaks.

Goat Creek clear cut in 1996 (photography Gordon Petersen, courtesy of Canadian Parks and Wilderness Society); alpine meadow at the base of Mount McGladrey.

## Access

### from Crowsnest Pass:

Drive south on the Lynx (Sartoris) Road from Blairmore, crossing a cattle guard at the top of Willoughby ridge before dropping to Lynx Creek. After crossing a bridge over Lynx Creek, drive another 1.25 km and look for a logging road.

### from Beaver Mines:

Drive south on Highway 774 and take the Castle recreation road west (just before the Castle River bridge), turning left at the T junction to the Lynx Creek Road (11.4 km). Take the Lynx Creek Road north for 10 km, crossing two bridges on the way. The trailhead is the first main logging road you see heading west after you cross the second bridge. Park at the junction of Goat Creek Road and Lynx Creek Road.

## Route Description

The trail starts with a gradual ascent on wide dirt road and immediately swings south for 500 m before once again heading west. The first 2 km are gently rolling through open terrain, with views of extensive damage from the Lost Creek fire visible in all directions.

After just over 2 km the trail splits. Take right fork toward Mount McGladrey and the North Goat Creek headwaters. (The left fork, heavily used by ATVs, takes you to South Goat Creek and farther to Lost Creek.) Follow the double track for a further 500 m through a large logged clearing offering a clear view of McGladrey. Once at the west end of the clearing, the trail begins a gradual ascent. Stay straight and do not take the spur to the right.

The next 2 km are pretty straightforward, as you're travelling on a clearly defined trail ascending the forested bench above North Creek. Because this trail is not as widely used by ATVs, sections in mid-summer are choked with alder, dogwood and buckthorn. A "Trail Closed to ATVs" sign marks 4.5 km into the hike. The trail immediately becomes overgrown and harder to distinguish. Stay straight on a cutline through the burn, climbing over numerous dead snags. Within 200 m you arrive at a ford of North Goat Creek.

The trail appears to cross the creek at this point and head up the east shoulder of Mount Pengelly. Instead, stay on the north side of the creek. Persevere, stay near the bank, and a wildlife trail will show itself intermittently, finally opening up to the base of a rocky subalpine meadow. Cross a side creek and ascend along wildlife trail sharply to the top of the first knoll. The meadow levels off enough so you can choose your route up the bowl to the base of Mount McGladrey.

Opposite top: Double track through meadow; ATV access ends 4.5 km into hike as the trail becomes overgrown.
Below: Alpine bowl at base of Mount McGladrey; view of Goat Creek drainage and open slopes from logging in 1996. Prairie Bluff, Victoria Peak and Windsor Mountain are visible in the distance.

## Mount McGladrey
2758 m (9,050 ft.)
Origin of name unknown

## Mount Pengelly
2560 m (8,399 ft.)
Named in 1914. "Pengelly" was the maiden name of Alberta Land Surveyor A.J. Campbell's wife. Campbell was an assistant to Arthur Oliver (A.O.) Wheeler on the Alberta-British Columbia Interprovincial Boundary Survey. Although Mount McGladrey and Mount Pengelly are named, the taller peak to the north is not.

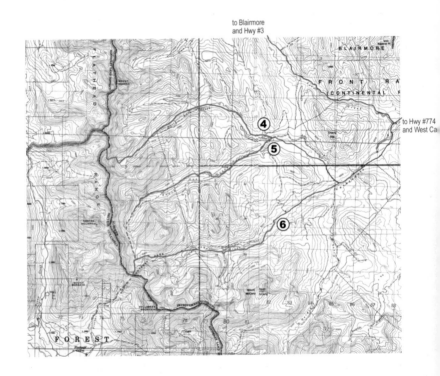

## 4.  NORTH LOST CREEK

| | |
|---|---|
| Distance: | 9.5 km to headwall; 11 km to tarn; 11.5 km to south ridge of Mt. Darrah |
| Rating: | moderate to difficult (if continuing to lake and ridge) |
| Time: | 3+ hrs. to head of valley (4+ to lake) |
| Start elevation: | 1495 m |
| End of trail: | 1861 m |
| Elevation at lake: | 2166 m |
| Elevation on ridge: | 2361 m |
| Max. elevation gain: | 866 m |
| Mode of travel: | bike and/or hike |
| Maps: | 82G/8 Beaver Mines, 82G/7 Flathead Ridge |
| Terrain: | dirt track, single track, steep scramble to lake and to ridge, scramble to ridge |
| Note: | 4WD users on early sections. |

## Overview and Comments

This is probably the most rewarding and variable hike and scramble along the eastern slopes of the Flathead Range. Like the North Kootenay and South Lost Creek trails the hike gets more interesting the farther in you go. What makes this hike rewarding is the picturesque bowl at the head of the valley as well as accessible high-elevation lakes and ridge tops. Unlike with South Lost Creek, the bowl here is steeper, tighter and more defined.

The high slopes of Mount Darrah are prime mountain goat habitat. The Forest Service census in summer 2005 counted 85 goats along the Divide, with the highest concentration being on and around Mount Darrah. A team from the Interprovincial Boundary Commission made the first ascent of Mount Darrah in 1914.

View from saddle above a small alpine lake looking at the west face of Mt. Darrah's south ridge.

## Access

*from Crowsnest Pass:*
Drive south on either the Sartoris Road from Blairmore or the Adanac Road from Hillcrest to the Lynx Creek recreation area campground.

*from Beaver Mines:*
Drive south on Highway 774 and take the Castle recreation road west (just before the Castle River bridge) for 2 km, turning left at the T junction to the Lynx Creek recreation area.

At 1 km south of the Lynx Creek recreation area campground, take a rough road (CAMP #56) that parallels the Carbondale River. Drive 4.5 km

Panorama of Mt. Darrah from North Lost Creek.

and take the right fork; then drive another 4 km on another rough section of road (Lost Creek Road) that parallels the lower reach of Lost Creek. After crossing a bridge the road forks again. The south (left) fork will take you to a winter shelter built by the Pincher Creek and Crowsnest Pass snowmobile clubs. The right fork is the beginning of the North Lost Creek trail.

## Route Description

The trail begins by climbing gently to the open bench on the north side of North Lost Creek. Immediately you come to a secondary trail heading north, stay straight for the next 1.75 km. Like the beginning of all the hikes in the Lost Creek Area, the rolling terrain above the bench land was severely burned by the 2003 Lost Creek fire. With the lack of needle cover it is easy to see the maze of logging roads traversing the surrounding hillsides. There is also plenty of opportunity to look ahead to Mount Darrah and Mount Pengelly to its right, as well as back to Willoughby Ridge.

After 2 km a second trail heads to the Goat Creek valley. Stay straight and gradually descend. Cross a rickety bridge over North Lost Creek (2.4 km). The trail then climbs back to the bench and levels out. This section can be boggy in the early summer.

Once past the bridge, the trail makes a turn to the west, paralleling the creek for a short distance. An old logging road forks left 1 km farther along. Stay straight on the double track, as it eventually winds its way through a fresh trail cut close to the creek bank.

At 3.5 km, cross North Lost Creek for the second time and climb back up onto the bench. Quickly a major trail junction (CAMP #35) appears. The road heading straight north is a well-used 4WD route to Goat Creek. Stay straight. Within 500 m you arrive at a third crossing – this time a tributary of North Lost Creek. The area is a mix of open meadow, gravel bars and burn. Shortly after this crossing, a trail accessing the old, washed-out route on the south bank veers off to the left. This old trail is still used by snowmobilers to access a cutline heading south over to the South Lost Creek drainage. Instead, stay straight and come to another major trail (4.5 km) heading due north. This is the major access route to the north bowl below Mount Darrah.

Stay straight as the trail begins another short ascent through more burned forest. The trail levels out after 100 m only to begin another short ascent. For the next few kilometres the trail rolls and bends through heavy forest. Because of the larger trees that flank this stretch, the trail holds snow longer and can be muddy, especially in early summer. ATVs have played havoc in this area, especially at 6.25 km, where a number of detours have been plowed through the bush, around the steeper, more eroded parts.

After another short, steep climb out of the forest, you emerge onto a logged-out bench at the base of a side slope. Reenter the forest, hiking up and down but gaining elevation overall. The trail's width has ballooned with heavier ATV use. At 7.25 km, cross a stream coming from thick forest cover. This stream drains two small alpine lakes below Mount Darrah. The stream, a snowmobile route, is the most direct way to these lakes, but the 1 km bushwhack makes it a discouraging option. Instead, stay the course. Flanked by six-metre spruce trees and the odd clearing, the next 1 km is straight with a slight uphill grade. The trail

Cirque at end of main trail. Scrambling up the headwall will take you to a small alpine lake that remains partially frozen year-round.

Limestone outcrops make for an interesting climb to the lake.

then takes a turn right and climbs though a mature spruce and fir forest, opening up to a picturesque alpine bowl. From here the trail's end is easily visible, straight ahead at the base of a 150 m waterfall cascading down the steep headwall.

This is one of the more picturesque alpine bowls in the Castle Wilderness and you might be content to explore its lower slopes. Or try the challenging ascent up the north slope to a small alpine lake at the base of the 300 m (1,000 ft.) rock face. Expending the time and energy climbing to the lake is well worth it.

### Getting to the lake:

Begin a tricky, angled ascent to right of the cascade, skirting further right around cliff bands. This scramble is steep and wet as you gain 180 m over the first 250 m. Once above the first set of cliff bands, the terrain levels out and the route choices are more obvious – basically straight up the rocky meadow for the next 350 m to the tarn. The hiking, although steep, is relatively easy and pleasant as you pass by and climb over craggy, odd-shaped boulders and outcrops that dot the steep meadow.

An optional ascent is to pick your way along scattered animal trails through the rocks further to the right and keep switching back west until you reach the lake. Some cliffs are impassable, so route finding is necessary.

Route from lake to the ridge along the Continental Divide; looking back down to the tarn; looking from ridge to alpine lake on B.C. side.

The lake is a wonderful example of a high-elevation tarn (2166 m). Sandpaper-rough limestone boulders scoured by ice and water are crammed with a variety of alpine flowers: stonecrop, moss campion, saxifrage and others. The 300 m headwall casts a constant, cooling shadow that sustains a year-round floe of ice coloured by purple algae.

The route to the saddle is obvious from a shoulder above the lake – a steep, well-travelled trail 300 m up the scree to the north. On the way up one might hear and see marmots or mountain goats. From a small saddle on the ridge there are views of the knife-edged south ridge of Mount Darrah and a small alpine lake on the B.C. side below.

**Exploring Beyond**

At 5 km into the hike, take the right fork and follow the trail as it takes you to a bowl below the main, north peak of Mount Darrah. From this bowl it is possible to continue southwest over a shoulder and down into Lost Lake meadows.

### Mount Darrah

2755 m (9,039 ft.)

Named in 1916. Captain Darrah was the astronomer attached to the British Bounday Commission, which delineated the border from the Pacific to the Rockies. The mountain is also known as "Gable Mountain" in the Interprovincial Boundary Survey Atlas. It was likely remamed because of the existence of another Gable Mountain in the Red Deer River Valley.

## 5. SOUTH LOST CREEK

| | |
|---|---|
| Distance: | 8.5 km to end of trail; 10.7 km to North Kootenay Saddle |
| Time: | 3.0 + hrs to head of valley (4.5+ hrs. to saddle) |
| Rating | moderate (difficult if accessing saddle) |
| Start elevation: | 1492 m |
| Elevation at trail end: | 1742 m |
| Elevation at North Kootenay Saddle: | 1940 m |
| Max. elevation gain: | 448 m |
| Terrain: | dirt track (logging road) through meadows and old burn areas, three major fords, one bridge crossing, some wet springs |
| Maps: | 82G/8 Beaver Mines, 82G/7 Flathead Ridge |
| Note: | Some ATV use in the lower sections of the trail. |

### Overview and Comments

This trail is not the most inspiring of routes in the Castle Wilderness, but what it lacks in views and high alpine terrain it makes up in the abundance of wildflowers, especially in the Lost Creek fire burn areas early on in the hike. The steep east face of Centre Mountain is impressive, though less so than other headwalls along the Flathead Range such as Mounts Darrah, Pengelly and McGladrey.

Like North Kootenay Pass and North Lost Creek hikes, this route starts farther from the Divide than hikes found to the north and is therefore longer.

The headwaters of South Lost Creek are heavily vegetated, making access and further route finding difficult.

### Access

*from Crowsnest Pass:*
Drive south on either the Sartoris Road from Blairmore or the Adanac Road from Hillcrest to the Lynx Creek recreation area campground.

*from Beaver Mines:*
Drive south on Highway 774 and take the Castle recreation road west (just before the Castle River bridge) for 2 km, turning left at the T junction to the Lynx Creek recreation area

At 1 km south of the Lynx Creek recreation area campground, take a rough road (CAMP #56) that parallels the Carbondale River. Drive 4.5

View of South Lost Creek headwaters from North Kootenay
Pass trail with Mount Darrah in the centre background.

km and take the right fork; then drive another 4 km on another rough
section of road that parallels the lower reach of Lost Creek. After crossing
a bridge the road forks again: take the left fork and park at the winter
shelter built by the Pincher Creek and Crowsnest Pass snowmobile clubs.

## Route Description

The trail begins by crossing a bridge over what is actually North Lost
Creek just before it flows into South Lost Creek. Less than a kilometre
past this bridge you come to another creek crossing. You have two choices
here: either a ramshackle bridge or the cold, shin-deep (in early summer)
water of South Lost Creek.

Immediately turn west on the main road. Once you reach the bench
above South Lost Creek, the going is flat and easy on a wide-open double
track through meadows and light forest cover, much of it burned in the
Lost Creek fire of 2003. There are plenty of opportunities to look ahead to
your final destination: Centre Mountain's main, pyramidal peak, flanked
by its eastern headwall. But it is also a pleasure to look down at the bright
patches of arnica and daisy and later on in the summer the fireweed
blooming among the fire-blackened pine and spruce.

Fireweed and ox-eye daisy; trail follows south bench of South Lost Creek.

After 2.5 km there is a major cutline heading south. Stay straight and the trail drops you back down to creek level. After 1 km you'll come to a signed trail (a route used by snowmobilers to access the Carbondale River valley) veering to the left and a stream running across the main track that is wet year-round. Instead, keep right. The trail continues to drop for another 500 m, turning north into a nice grassy floodplain meadow and eventually crosses South Lost Creek back to the north bank.

The trail, still a double track at this point, inclines slightly for 1 km through burned spruce and fir forest. Centre Mountain and its broad east ridge fill the panorama ahead. Side streams washing over the trail have left it wet and rocky in sections but it is still easy going. Soon after this section a signed secondary trail heads off to the right (north). This cutline takes the user, usually ATVers and snowmobilers, over to the North Lost Creek drainage.

Go 500 m farther and you come to another major, signed fork in the trail. The left route, an older road heading down and across South Lost Creek, is now washed out after 250 m. Instead, stay straight as the trail starts up a steady incline onto a bench below a cliff face. Looking across the valley to the south you can see sections of the old trail mixed in with old logging roads and washouts. It looks like this might still provide a route over to Carbondale Valley and North Kootenay Pass for the intrepid explorer.

Cascade near the end of hike; after 6 km take right fork.

After another kilometre you cross a stream with a pleasant cascade coming out of a hanging valley below the northeast ridge of Centre Mountain. Looking up as you approach this point from back on the trail, there appears to be an obvious route traversing the north shoulder into this side valley, but no trail entrance makes itself apparent after crossing the stream. With some serious bushwacking it might be possible to access this trail and the valley.

After you cross the stream a short, sharp incline brings you to an old logging staging area offering a clear view of the saddle over into the North Kootenay Pass. Continue on up a double track winding through open spruce, fir and pine. At the base of an avalanche slope the main trail ends after 8.5 km.

South portion of Centre Mountain's east ridge with saddle into North Kootenay Pass to the left.

## Exploring Beyond

The end of this trail is a letdown, but it is possible to extend the hike with some route finding and access the saddle between the South Lost Creek and the Carbondale drainages.

A single track continues for another 1 km, taking you back down to the creek, but it disappears into thick bush with more ground cover than you will want to negotiate: alder, skunkweed, fireweed. A number of game trails look promising, but it is easier to stay high, picking your way through stumps, rocks and stubby alder up to the more open scree slopes below the headwall and traverse for another 2 km up to the saddle.

## 6.  NORTH KOOTENAY PASS

| | |
|---|---|
| Distance: | 9.5 km to boundary; 10.2 km to lookout over B.C. |
| Time: | 3.5+ hrs. to pass |
| Rating: | moderate to difficult |
| Start elevation: | 1475 m |
| Elevation at pass: | 2050 m |
| End elevation: | 2068 m |
| Max. elevation gain: | 593 m |
| Terrain: | open dirt road/double track with creek crossings, benchland, subalpine, alpine |
| Mode of travel: | bike and/or hike |
| Maps: | 82G/8 Beaver Mines, 82G/7 Flathead Ridge |
| Note: | You may find ATVs and motorbikes in the area, especially on weekends. |

### Description and Comments

This was one of the main routes used by the Ktunaxa over the Continental Divide. Following directions from the Ktunaxa, Thomas Blakiston crossed the North Kootenay Pass in August 1858. Reporting back to expedition leader John Palliser, he thought a railway would be feasible but the notion was rejected by the Canadian Government owing to concerns about security: the pass was too close to the Canada/us border.

A plaque and provincial boundary marker add to this route's sense of history. And with the jagged southeast wall of Centre Mountain, the tight notch through the pass and views into the Flathead Valley, this hike ends better than it begins.

Once the domain of aboriginal hunters and explorers, this route is now one of the most utilized ATV trails in the Castle. Despite its length and the possibility of motorized users, North Kootenay Pass is still one of the easiest and most straightforward routes over the Continental Divide. And if you want to bike the less exciting initial flat section, the length will not seem so daunting.

## Access

### from Crowsnest Pass:

Drive south on Sartoris Road from Blairmore or Adanac Road from Hillcrest to the Lynx Creek recreation area campground.

### from Beaver Mines:

Drive south on Highway 774 for 12.5 km and take the Castle recreation road west (just before the Castle River bridge) for 2 km. Turn left at the T junction and drive to the Lynx Creek recreation area. One kilometre south of the Lynx Creek recreation area campground, take a rough road (CAMP #56) that parallels the Carbondale River for 7 km. Park your vehicle 1 km from CAMP trail marker #29, where the road ends by a narrow wooden bridge.

The hike starts by crossing the bridge. Despite what outdated guidebooks say and old topographic maps show, you want to be on south side of the Carbondale River, so avoid the temptation to continue straight ahead after the bridge. (This trail ends abruptly 4 km later in dense bush.) Instead,

The start of the North Kootenay Pass trail is a makeshift wooden bridge; go left after crossing and head down to Carbondale River and cross a second bridge.

turn left immediately after crossing and hike 100 m to another bridge, built after the 1995 flood, that allows you to cross the Carbondale River easily.

After the bridge, the trail swings southwest, winding and climbing slightly on a wide dirt road through mixed forest and meadow until it reaches the open bench on the south side of Carbondale creek. You soon arrive at two successive bridges, both crossing deep-cut streams coming down from Mount McCarty. Less than 1 km further there is another crossing, but this time there is no bridge. The trail instead picks a route across the boulder-strewn streambed.

Less than 1 km farther another route (camp trail #28) veers left up the Macdonald Creek headwaters and to a steep pass over the southeast ridge of Hollebeke Mountain. Stay straight for North Kootenay Pass. A little past this trail junction, Macdonald Creek crosses the road on the way to its confluence with the Carbondale River. This is an easy crossing by mid-summer but can be a small torrent in the spring. After the crossing the trail bends its way back up through thick vegetation to the bench.

There really isn't much to this initial part of the hike, barely gaining 100 m of elevation over the first 4 km. You're hiking on wide open road, passing old cut blocks with plenty of daisy, fireweed and alder. Views of Centre Mountain and its east wall can be seen further up the valley. The road stays along the bench for another 1 km then eventually drops back down to the Carbondale River. A large spruce has fallen over the river, providing a handy natural bridge over what might otherwise be a difficult ford in the early summer.

The trail, now down to a double track, snakes up the valley bottom through spruce/fir forest and emerges on the north bench, where it continues to ascend gradually for the next 2.5 km. Bright Indian paintbrush dots the steep slopes and rock outcrops as you pass the base of an unnamed ridge. The main track then takes a steep climb through another small stand of fir and spruce. Because of the grade and extensive use of ATVs, this section is a mess of loose rock and dirt. A gentler, less obvious route veers left just before this climb into a spring-fed, flower-choked meadow, eventually reconnecting with the main trail that traverses the meadow from above.

Accessing the saddle between the South Lost Creek and the Carbondale drainages, the higher, main route does afford views north along the eastern slopes of the Clark Range. A small, pretty meadow, now a place for illegal ATV use, offers nice views down into the South Lost Creek drainage and north where on a clear day the dominant peak of Mount Darrah is clearly visible. From this point you have a clear view of the relatively easy route snaking ahead across the rocky meadow at the base of Centre Mountain's east wall and on up into the notch through the pass. If you are lucky to have this alpine setting to your hiking selves, take the time to soak up the open views all around, listening for marmot.

> "Gradually the stream became less and less until after gaining considerable altitude it dwindled into a small quantity of water falling in a cascade. We now rose rapidly, the trees became smaller, and we soon reached the region of rock and alpine plants; here were some large patches of snow and a couple of ponds of clear water; we passed over a quantity of debris of hard gray limestone, of which the peaks on our right hand, namely N.W., were composed. As we were now clear of all shelter, we felt the cold damp east wind."
>
> — Thomas Blakiston

After 1 km you arrive at a plaque unveiled during a 1982 hike commemorating Blakiston's expedition. Less than 250 m farther, and 9.5 km into the hike, is the official pass at 2050 m, marked with a Provincial Boundary point. The trail continues through a windy, rocky notch, squeezed between the north ridge of Mt Hollebeke to the south and the jagged crags of Centre Mountain to the north. As you crest the notch, the views open west to the Flathead Valley, northwest to Mount Borsato and south to Hollebeke Mountain.

### Exploring beyond

The double track continues for another 5 km down to the headwaters of Pincher Creek (not to be confused with Pincher Creek, Alberta) and on to the Flathead Valley road. From the saddle between the South Lost Creek and the Carbondale drainages, take an unmarked route north following the lower

Clockwise from top: Cairn marks the actual provincial boundary;
looking northeast through pass from the B.C. side;
view west through notch at North Kootenay Pass;
jagged southeast ridge of Centre Mountain.

talus slopes of Centre Mountain for 2.5 km down into South Lost Creek and connecting with the well-used trail on the north side of the creek.

### Mount McCarty
2358 m (7,737 ft.)
Named in 1915. Located south of the headwaters of the Carbondale River, west of Gardiner Creek.

### Centre Mountain
2601 m (8,533 ft.)

### Hollebeke Mountain
2221 m (7,288 ft.)
Named in 1917. Hollebeke is a village in Belgium near the French border about five miles from Ypres. Canadian troops fought in and near Hollebeke during the First World War.

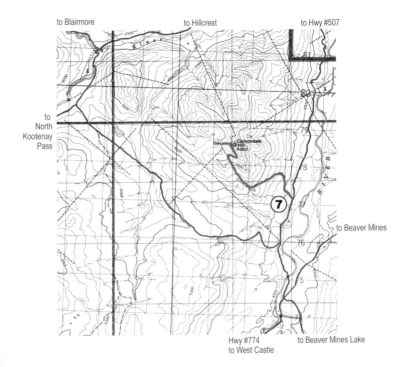

**Borsato Mountain**

2441 m (8,010 ft.)

Named in 1961 for Pte. Leno Borsato, from Michel, B.C. (a small mining town on the western side of Crowsnest Pass), who was killed on December 9, 1944, while serving with the Canadian Armed Forces.

## 7. CARBONDALE FIRE ROAD

| | |
|---|---|
| Distance: | 4 km to lookout |
| Time: | 1.5 hrs. |
| Rating: | easy |
| Start elevation: | 1354 m |
| End elevation: | 1800 m |
| Max. elevation gain: | 446 m |
| Terrain: | dirt road, forest cover, open ridge |
| Mode of travel: | bike or hike |
| Maps: | 82G/8 Beaver Mines |
| Note: | Road to fire lookout. Do not disturb lookout occupants. |

### Overview and Comments

This hike or bike follows the road up Carbondale Hill to the fire lookout. The first 2.75 km through the trees are relatively uneventful. Once you are out of the trees and onto the open ridge, though, the view, as one might imagine from the vantage point of a fire lookout, becomes a panorama of the major peaks in the Castle, from Victoria to Coulthard. This is a good hike if you only have half a day or want a sunset hike.

The hike up the Carbondale fire road is leisurely until near the summit, where the road makes a series of switchbacks; the view from the summit looking south is one of the best in the Castle.

## Access

Drive 13 km south from Beaver Mines on Highway 774 and turn right onto the Castle River road (before the bridge crossing Castle River). Follow this for 1.5 km. Cross the cattle guard and drive another 1 km. Park by a locked gate on the north side of the road.

## Route Description

Follow the road through mixed forest of aspen, spruce and pine. After 1.6 km there is an opening and a ledge with views down the West Castle Valley. One kilometre later, after a switchback and an open gate, the trees thin out, and from this point on, the route remains open and exposed. It can often be windy. After another major switchback, the lookout becomes visible. The top of the ridge is only minutes away.

# West Castle Valley Hikes

## 8.  BARNABY RIDGE – SOUTHFORK LAKES

| | |
|---|---|
| Distance: | 3.8 km to first lake; 4.75 km to upper lakes |
| Time: | 2.5 hrs. to lower lake |
| Rating: | moderate day hike or backpack |
| Start elevation: | 1410 m |
| Elevation at lower lake: | 1922 m; upper lakes, 2040 m |
| Max. elevation gain: | 630 m |
| Terrain: | river crossing, bush, single track, subalpine |
| Mode of travel: | hike |
| Maps: | 82G/8 Beaver Mines |
| Note: | Major ford of West Castle River, some route finding necessary. |

## Overview and Comments

A major ford of West Castle River starts this hike. The river can be waist deep, cold and fast-running in the early summer. Best to leave this hike for later in the summer when the water level has dropped. Finding the main trail after crossing the river can be frustrating. Before starting out, look to the shoulder leading up Barnaby Ridge and set your bearings

182

to Beaver Mines

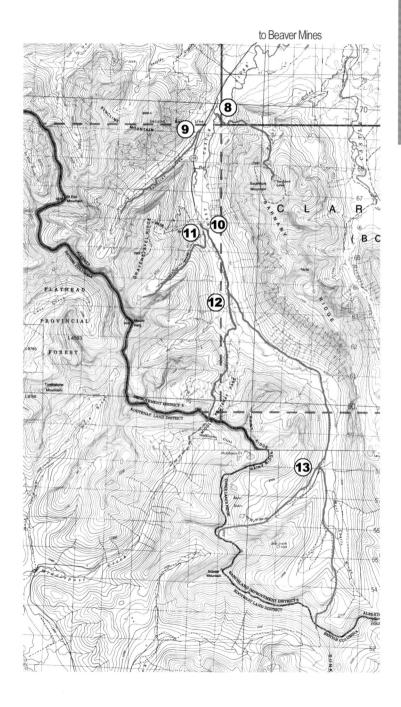

on the trail etched in the open slope. The steep ascent up the north shoulder of Barnaby Ridge is gruelling and seems to take longer than it should. Persevere, for the reward of three alpine lakes is worth the effort. Wonderful larch forest above the lakes on back side of Barnaby Ridge make this a great early fall hike.

In the 1990s mountain goats were released in an attempt to re-establish a population on Barnaby Ridge. The goats have since moved on. The lower lake was once stocked with non-native golden trout. The restocking program has ended and the trout are in decline. In 1938 a major fire rushed through Middle Kootenay Pass, leaving a wonderful array of twisted snags all along the steep upper shoulder.

**Access**

Drive 18.5 km south from Beaver Mines on Highway 774. Look for a potholed dirt road heading left into the aspen, toward the West Castle River. Follow this for another 400 m and then turn left again to an open random camping area next to the river, and park there.

**Route Description**

Start by following the trail through the willows around an elbow in the river until it ends at a suitable place to cross. Ford the river and head straight into the bush on the most travelled route. After 150 m, the route through the bush finally emerges onto a more prominent trail. Turn left. Follow for less than 200 m until the trail forks right and heads straight toward the shoulder of Barnaby Ridge. This section has been marked with flagging tape, but don't rely on this. You should be able to look ahead and see the route up the shoulder. Before you get there, however, the trail takes a hard left, eventually crossing a deep-cut stream after a further 150 m. Cross the stream and turn right. You are now about to start the main ascent, beginning with a series of switchbacks through lodgepole pine.

After 250 m, emerge from trees and begin an even steeper ascent up loose shale. The next kilometres can be hot, dry and windy. This is by far

View of the lower lake from the trail to the upper lakes.

the most difficult section of the hike, gaining more than 300 m in elevation. Take time to rest and scan the panorama across the West Castle Valley: Castle Resort ski hill to the south, Syncline Mountain straight across. If you look below you should be able to see where you parked your vehicle.

Finally the trail levels off and enters the shade of a spruce forest for 1 km, dropping slightly through the trees. A final short ascent leads to an opening where Barnaby Creek flows from the lower lake, now less than 100 m straight ahead. It's worthwhile to take a swim to cool off after the hot climb. Winds coming down from the upper basin can be strong at times. Skirt the lake and hike the final 500 m to the upper basin and its two lakes, ascending through steep sections of dwarf spruce and willow and over open, rocky, juniper-covered bench land.

A rock cliff to the north offers good views of the two lakes and Southfork Mountain. There are rudimentary trails to take you around both lakes. The shallow water along the shore is warmer than you'd expect. Winds are often gusty here, but trees along the east side of the middle lake offer cover for camping.

185

The final 500 m route to the upper basin.
The ridge between the two upper lakes.

## Exploring Beyond

Camping in the lower or upper basin will give you time to explore the upper slopes of Barnaby Ridge. Some 3.5 km from Southfork Mountain is a lookout over a dramatic hanging valley and a small, unnamed alpine lake above Grizzly Creek Valley.

### Barnaby Ridge
2471 m (8,106 ft.)
The high point on the northern end of Barnaby Ridge is known as Southfork Mountain. The ridge is 8 km long. Barnaby Ridge with Southfork Mountain as its highest peak is the first major landform differentiating the West Castle River from the south branch of the Castle River.

### Southfork Mountain
2330 m (7,645 ft.)
The Castle River was known as the "South Fork" of the Oldman River and later as "Southfork River." Part I of the Interprovincial Boundary Survey (1917) reads: "The term 'North Fork' was applied by (George Dawson) to distinguish this branch of 'Old Man River' from the 'South Fork' of the same stream, which heads on the east side of the watershed not very far north of South Kootenay Pass and joins the 'North Fork' a few miles northwest of Pincher Station on the Canadian Pacific Railway. The name 'South Fork Old Man River' was subsequently changed to 'Southfork River' and again, quite recently, to Castle River. For the northern branch, the term 'North Fork' has been dropped and it is now known as 'Oldman River.'"

## 9. SYNCLINE BROOK

| | |
|---|---|
| Distance: | 4 km to swimming hole |
| Time: | 1.5+ hrs. |
| Rating: | easy |
| Start elevation: | 1380 m |
| End elevation: | 1540 m |
| Max. elevation gain: | 160 m |
| Terrain: | creek crossing, double track, single track |
| Mode of travel: | hike |
| Maps: | 82G/8 Beaver Mines |
| Note: | Flooding has washed out early sections of trail; some minor route finding necessary. |

### Overview and Comments

If you only have half a day this is a relatively easy route. This hike, barely climbing above the valley bottom, has four shallow creek crossings. The trail follows an old 4wD road that is no longer accessible for ATV users. The 1995 flood reclaimed much of the flood plain and parts of the original trail. There is a small chute with a shallow swimming hole at the end of a 4 km hike. Thick bush prevents exploration to the head of the valley.

The many lush avalanche slopes along Syncline Mountain's south ridge provide good bear habitat, and signs of bear in the valley can be numerous. The upper ledges and cliffs of Syncline are also prime mountain goat habitat, so it is well worth packing binoculars.

### Access

Take Highway 774 and drive 20 km south from Beaver Mines. Pull off and park in the clearing to the right just before the bridge crossing Syncline Brook.

### Route Description

Start by crossing over a berm built to obstruct ATV use and follow an old roadbed through a mix of trees and open meadow. After 500 m turn right, and the double track makes a slight incline before dropping to a gravel flood plain with large cottonwoods. Here the trail for the next 200 m becomes less clear. Stay on the north bank, taking the most obvious

Spionkop Creek below St. Eloi;
rocky chute at end of the hike.

track through the trees for 100 m before crossing the stream flowing into Syncline Brook. Do not take the trail heading up to the right. Instead, stay tight to the north bank of Syncline Brook and pick up the ATV track again as it climbs to a bench at the base of an avalanche slope. With binoculars, scan the upper slopes and cliffs on Syncline Mountain for goats.

Cross a washout and continue to a second, larger washout 350 m farther. Follow a trail down the washout and cross Syncline Brook. Pick up the trail on the south bank that continues up the valley, crossing Syncline Brook again after only 50 m. Now back on the north side of the creek, follow the wide track for 400 m and cross Syncline yet again.

After this third crossing the trail heads up a steep embankment. From here continue up the bench on the south side of Syncline Brook. Other than a short stretch of thick alder, this last 500 m to a final crossing of Syncline is open and relatively easy hiking with views of the ridge between Syncline Mountain and St. Eloi Mountain at the head of the valley. At the crossing the brook rushes alongside a rocky ledge. A pool at the base of the chute is a nice place to cool off.

While it looks like the trail may continue to the head of the valley, it quickly becomes overgrown. It is possible to hike another 500 m to a waterfall coming off St. Eloi Mountain. But even that requires a bushwack through thick vegetation to get to the base.

## Syncline Mountain
2441 m (8009 ft.)

Syncline Mountain was named during the Interprovincial Boundary Survey in 1917 after surveyors noted "a very apparent physical feature." Syncline is the geological term for a trough-shaped fold in layers of rock. If softer rocks are in the fold's core, they will erode to form a valley. If the inner layers are harder, erosion carves them into a peak instead. Syncline Mountain has three high points, but only the eastern peak is visible from Syncline Brook valley. The three peaks form a hanging valley on the northeast face containing the headwaters of Suicide Creek.

## St. Eloi Mountain
2504 m (8216 ft.)

Located on the Continental Divide at the head of Syncline Brook and St. Eloi Brook. Canadian troops fought near the village of St. Eloi, France, during the First World War and the peak was named in 1917.

## 10. HAIG LAKE

| | |
|---|---|
| Distance: | 4 km |
| Time: | 2 hrs. |
| Rating: | moderate day hike |
| Start elevation: | 1417 m |
| High elevation: | 1813 m |
| Lake elevation: | 1782 m |
| Max. elevation gain: | 396 m |
| Terrain: | logging road, ski slope, double track, subalpine |
| Mode of travel: | hike |
| Maps: | 82G/8 Beaver Mines |
| Note: | Logging on the slopes of Haig Ridge has rerouted the lower section of the hike. |

### Overview and Comments

Mount Haig, with its stratified pyramid shape, is one of the most recognizable peaks in the Castle. The hike to the lake at the base of the mountain's north face is also one of the region's most popular. Although not the most picturesque hike, the route to Haig Lake is short and direct, making the lake readily accessible. Less than 200 m across and with year-round snow along its shore, Haig Lake offers a refreshing swim on a hot

189

Haig Lake looking northeast out toward Barnaby Ridge.

day. The upper valley slopes are also favourite grizzly and black bear habitat, especially in late summer when huckleberries are ripe.

Recent logging on the lower slopes of Haig Ridge and the expansion of infrastructure at the base of the ski hill have made a mess of the lower section of the trail. Originally starting up from the lower reaches of Gravenstafel (Haig) Brook, hikers must now follow the temporary signage through the logged area before reaching the original trail.

**Access**

Drive south of Beaver Mines to the ski hill and park at far south end of the parking lot.

**Route Description**

Follow the chalet road from the southwest corner straight for 250 m until you come to a roped-off logging area. Cross under the rope and follow the logging road for a further 200 m until you come to a marked trail veering up to the right. This short section levels off at a log-staging area. Turn sharply to the right, cross the staging area and continue on the old section of access road until it crosses an unused ski run (part of an older plan to expand the ski hill onto Haig Ridge). From here turn left and head up alongside the ski run. After 500 m of steep slogging, the ski run veers to the left while the trail stays straight and crosses under an avalanche warning rope. After a short distance, you lose elevation before beginning a steady ascent to the lake. At various points there are views to the south slopes of Gravenstafel Ridge.

The trail for the next 500 m cuts straight through young spruce stand with views ahead to the north face of Mount Haig. The shady sections hold snow well into summer and can be muddy. After levelling off, the trail emerges onto open bench and then follows the rocky base of Haig Ridge before descending the moraine to the lake.

The urge to explore the Haig Basin is understandable. Huckleberries and wildflowers cover the south slopes of Gravenstafel Ridge. Be careful of occasional rock falls from Haig's steep north face.

**Exploring beyond**

For an alternative route down, traverse the open southeast-facing slopes on the west side of Haig Lake. Do not drop to the creek and you will eventually hit the ski-out trail, which will lead you to the base of the ski hill.

Logging has made a mess of the original trailhead;
cutline trail to Haig Lake.

## Mount Haig

2610 m (8,563 ft.)

Located on the Continental Divide at the heads of Haig Creek, Cate Creek and Gravenstafel Brook. Clark Range. Named in 1862 for Captain R.W. Haig, who was the chief astronomer and senior military officer for the British Boundary Commission (1858–1862), which surveyed the international border from the Pacific to the Rockies.

## 11. MIDDLE KOOTENAY PASS

| | |
|---|---|
| Distance: | 8 km to pass |
| Time: | 2.5 hrs. to pass |
| Rating: | moderate day hike |
| Start elevation: | 1416 m |
| Pass elevation: | 1920 m |
| High elevation: | 1936 m – lookout into B.C. |
| Max. elevation gain: | 520 m |
| Terrain: | open 4WD road, double track, subalpine |
| Mode of travel: | hike and/or bike |
| Maps: | 82G/8 Beaver Mines |
| Note: | Major ATV route. Although ATVs are not allowed past the 3.75 km mark, tracks indicate use near and at the pass. |

## Overview and Comments

Within the Castle, Middle Kootenay Pass is the most straightforward route up to and over the Continental Divide. Although the Ktunaxa travelled over South Kootenay Pass (located between Waterton Lakes National Park and the Akamina-Kisenina Provincial Park in B.C.) their use of Middle Kootenay is less certain.

A road built to a well site in the 1970s, something the Ktunaxa obviously didn't have, has made this a popular route for ATV users. The road provides an easy and open, if uninteresting, trail, but it does get more interesting as you approach the Divide. A major fire in 1938 swept through the pass, leaving open alpine meadows choked with beargrass and penstemon. The trail over the pass side leads down to the Flathead Valley.

## Access

From Beaver Mines drive south on Highway 774 to the Castle Mountain Resort. Either park in the snowmobile staging area to the north of the ski hill and bike from here or continue in your vehicle. The road is rough but driveable. Continue past the ski hill on the West Castle road and cross the West Castle River bridge. Less than 3 km south of the ski hill you arrive at a major fork in an open meadow. From the meadow it is possible to set your bearings, with views of Mount Haig and the flat-topped Rainy Ridge. Park your vehicle in the clearing off the road and begin hiking or continue to bike.

## Route Description

Whether hiking or biking, take the right-hand fork heading west toward the Pass and immediately cross the bridge over the West Castle River. Cross a second bridge over a small tributary. The road parallels the West

The last kilometre to Middle Kootenay Pass is a leisurely stroll through scrub subalpine and alpine meadows.

Castle River for less than a kilometre, eventually turning right and ascending, with views ahead of the south face of Mount Haig. Continue to gradually gain elevation as the road turns back to the south and keeps heading straight for the next few kilometres.

Less than 3 km from crossing the West Castle River, the road levels out at an open staging area. There is an old well site in the clearing to the left. From here there are views of Barnaby Ridge east across the West Castle Valley and of Rainy Ridge to the south. The road over the next 500 m is narrower and steeper with loose rock and erosion from heavy ATV use.

Next you arrive at a barrier intended to prevent ATVs from accessing the Pass, although it's easy to see ATV tracks skirting around the barrier. From the gate it is possible to see a road winding up to the pass and an unnamed peak ahead. After passing the barrier, cross a small stream flowing from a pretty alpine meadow, and 200 m later a cascading

Above: View through Middle Kootenay Pass.
Opposite, clockwise from top left: the first bridge over the
West Castle River, with Rainy Ridge mountain to the south;
ATVs have roughened the trail along the way;
ATV barrier before Middle Kootenay Pass;
a cascade crosses the road to the Pass.

195

View of the main peak on Rainy Ridge.

mountain stream crosses the trail. Some caution is necessary because the rocks can be slippery. From here the road continues to wind and climb through a nice fir stand for another kilometre before taking a sharp left and finally levelling off.

From this first open plateau there are nice views back down the Castle Valley: Syncline Mountain to the north; far to the north through the Castle Valley, the Livingstone Range; Barnaby Ridge across the valley; and Rainy Ridge immediately ahead. The remaining 750 m to the pass is an open, easy, up-and-down hike that winds through old burn and alpine meadows full of beargrass and penstemon.

The actual pass is nothing more than a shale saddle with easy access to the ridge tops on either side. A short ascent up Rainy Ridge leads to views of the headwaters of Middle Pass Creek and a cluster of small subalpine lakes in a basin below the ridge.

### Exploring Beyond

From the pass the road winds down to Middle Pass Creek trail, accessing the lakes and then continuing for another 5 km to Flathead Road.

**Rainy Ridge**

2454 m (8,050 ft.)

Named in 1958. Located on the Continental Divide between West Castle River and the head of Middlepass Creek; southeast buttress of Middle Kootenay Pass; northeast of Three Lakes Ridge. High annual precipitation.

## 12. THREE LAKES RIDGE

| | |
|---|---|
| Distance: | 14 km to South Castle road; 4.0 km to Table Mountain summit |
| Time: | 4+ hrs. to ridge (cycling the first 7.5 km) |
| Rating: | difficult and long day hike |
| Start elevation: | 1416 m |
| High elevation: | 2440 m at peak north of saddle |
| Max. elevation gain: | 1032 m |
| Terrain: | 4WD road, double track, single track, subalpine, alpine |
| Mode of travel: | hike and bike |
| Maps: | 82G/8 Beaver Mines; 82G/1 Sage Creek |
| Notes: | Major ATV route along the West Castle road. A barrier 6 km from the first major fork restricts motorized use beyond this point. Routes farther up the West Castle Valley get more precipitation than those down the valley. Snow can linger well into summer. |

**Overview and Comments**

This is a rarely travelled route between Scarpe Mountain and Rainy Ridge, accessing the Continental Divide. While the name suggests an alpine lake destination, the ridge along the Divide is actually more rewarding, offering a wonderful vantage point from which to watch, with binoculars, resident mountain goats on the steep northwest face of Scarpe. There is one readily accessible lake on this route – the middle of three lakes, hence the name. A larger lake resides in an alpine bowl to the north, while a third, smaller lake is to the south, situated in the next drainage up on the southeast ridge of Scarpe

Once off the West Castle road the trail is overgrown owing to lack of use but still relatively easy to follow. The head of the valley below the lake was logged some time ago. This basin is also bear habitat – remote with plenty of forage. The route from the logged head of the valley to the upper basin is more difficult and requires some patience and route finding.

Scarpe Mountain from Three Lakes Ridge.
Mountain goats can be seen on the north face ledges.

## Access

From Beaver Mines drive south on Highway 774 to the Castle Mountain Resort. Either park in the snowmobile staging area just before the ski hill and bike from here or continue in your vehicle – the road is rough but driveable. Continue past the ski hill on the West Castle road and cross a wood bridge spanning the West Castle River. Less than 3 km south of the ski hill you arrive at a major fork in an open meadow. Park your vehicle in the clearing and take the left fork, continuing up the West Castle Valley road, either hiking or continuing to bike. It is another 7.5 km up the West Castle road to the actual trailhead.

## Route Description

From the fork, the road immediately ascends before levelling off. The next 3.5 km follows the rough, up-and-down West Castle road through forest and across numerous streams. You then begin to descend to the valley bottom, emerging onto an expansive clearing at the base of Barnaby Ridge. The road gradually bends south and 500 m later crosses a bridge over the West Castle River. Continue to follow the road lined with thick alder and steadily ascend for 2.5 km until you come to an ATV barrier.

Less than 100 m past the barrier the road splits. Take the right fork. (The left fork continues to the head of the West Castle Valley.) Follow the right fork for 250 m until you come to a small clearing. If you have biked to this point you'll want to stash your bike here. Climb steeply for 100 m before levelling off. Continue for the next 1.5 km on an overgrown single-track trail through mixed forest, crossing numerous mountain streams. This section seems to take longer than it should. Clearings through the thick vegetation offer views of the east ridge of Scarpe Mountain.

Finally you emerge into a clear cut at the head of the valley. The many old stumps give a good indication of the size of the trees harvested. The route becomes hard to distinguish. Take your bearings. You want to head toward a trail up the right side at the far end of the clearing. Stay to the right along the forest edge. Follow the most prominent trail for 250 m as it enters the forest. You'll come to a trail that heads to the right and deeper into the forest. This is the horse trail, a less interesting, alternative route to the lake.

Instead stay straight, following the edge of the clearing toward the head of the valley. You will have to scramble through some blowdown and cross a small creek. Pick up the wide trail (an old logging road) and head up a steep incline. After 250 m the trail levels off.

Follow a wide cutline toward the head of the basin. About 400 m after a slight right-hand dogleg, look for a spur trail heading up through

Clockwise from top left: trail can become overgrown from lack of use;
an old logging cutline leads to a basin below the ridge;
logged basin near headwaters.

thick bush to the right. It is easy to miss, but don't worry if you do. Stay straight for another 200 m until you come to the end of the cutline, next to a small moraine. The shoulder to the right divides this basin, with the lake on the other side. The most obvious route is a steep, angled ascent of the shoulder from the edge of the moraine. Once on the crest of the shoulder it is just a short descent to the lake, now in clear view. (To get

View of most readily accessed of the three lakes from the shoulder heading up the ridge.
Views of Barnaby Ridge, across the valley.

to a second, larger lake to the north, scramble up the north wall of the basin, skirting above the trees. From this ridge choose the safest route to the lake.)

### Accessing Three Lakes Ridge and Scarpe Mountain:

Follow the shoulder above the first lake for another kilometre to the high peak on Three Lakes Ridge. Stay on the leeward (right) edge of the shoulder to avoid the trees. Some 300 m below the peak a notch offers views down a tight valley to Middle Pass Creek. From here you can see the trail to Middle Kootenay Pass. From the peak it is an easy ridge walk to the saddle. Look for mountain goats on the north-face ledges of Scarpe Mountain.

From the saddle, angle back to your original route up along the shoulder above the lake and follow the same route down. If you drop too low straight down from the saddle, you will have to negotiate a very steep headwall below Scarpe Mountain.

### Three Lakes Ridge
2430 m (7,973 ft.)
The Interprovincial Boundary Survey established the "Three Lakes Camera Station" on the high point of this ridge.

### Scarpe Mountain
2591 m (8,501 ft.)
During the First World War, Canadian troops fought near the Scarpe River, which flows to the south of Vimy Ridge, France.

## 13. WEST CASTLE VALLEY ROAD

| | |
|---|---|
| Distance: | 15.5 km to Sunkist Ridge |
| Time: | 3.5+ hrs. cycling |
| Rating: | moderate to difficult |
| Start elevation: | 1420 m |
| Elevation: | 2180 m |
| Max. elevation gain: | 760 m |
| Terrain: | Well-used dirt road to overgrown logging road |
| Mode of travel: | Mountain bike and scramble, some bushwacking |
| Maps: | 82G/8 Beaver Mines; 82G/1 Sage Creek |
| Notes: | A barrier 6 km from the first major fork restricts motorized use beyond this point. |

### Overview and Comments

A 15 km dirt road follows the valley bottom from the ski hill to the West Castle River headwaters. The route is long and at times monotonous. There are a few minor climbs in the first 13 km, making this long section very bikeable. Farther up the valley the route becomes more overgrown and tedious. The final 2 km to the ridge are a scramble up an increasingly steep shoulder. Since the 1995 flood the major bridges have been repaired but there are at least two major tributaries to ford near the head of the valley. The route can be wet and muddy, especially early in the summer.

Some 100 m after the ATV barrier the trail splits.
La Coulotte Peak is in the distance to the left.

## Access

From Beaver Mines drive south on Highway 774 to the Castle Mountain
Resort. Either park in the snowmobile staging area to the north of the
resort and bike from here or continue driving (the road is rough but
driveable) for another 3 km past the ski hill until you come to a major
junction. Park in the large clearing off the road. The left fork is the one
that leads to the head of West Castle Valley. This is also the trailhead
for Three Lakes Ridge (see page 197). The right fork leads to Middle
Kootenay Pass (see page 192).

## Route Description

From the junction, the road south immediately ascends before levelling off.
The next 3.5 km follows the rough West Castle road up and down through
a mix of spruce, fir and poplar, crossing numerous streams. Descend to
the valley bottom, emerging onto an expansive clearing at the base of

Rainy Ridge from the West Castle road;
bridge below Barnaby Ridge.

Barnaby Ridge. The road gradually bends south and 500 m later crosses a bridge over the West Castle River. Steadily ascend for 2.5 km until you come to an ATV barrier (CAMP marker #17). From this point on, summer motorized vehicle use is prohibited. (Snow machines are permitted in the winter.) The road most of the way is lined with thick alder, although once in a while you get a glimpse of Sunkist Ridge and La Coulotte Peak at the head of the valley.

Just past the barrier, the road forks. Take the left fork and continue up the valley. Keeping to the right, instead of taking a trail dropping to and crossing the West Castle River, continue for another kilometre. At each of the next two junctions take the left fork and then cross a tributary. From here the trail gets increasingly overgrown and steep. If you want to reach the ridge, best to stash the bike and hike the rest of the way. Cross another tributary after 1.5 km and then begin the last 1.75 km up the steep shoulder to a section of Sunkist Ridge between Scarpe Mountain to the west and La Coulotte Peak to the east.

### Sunkist Ridge
2348 m (7,705 ft.)
Located on the Continental Divide, the ridge spans the 8 km from Scarpe Mountain to Sunkist Mountain. Named in 1958.

# SYNCLINE CROSS-COUNTRY SKI TRAILS

| | | | | |
|---|---|---|---|---|
| Distance: | 15 km network of trails | | Terrain: | Former ski trails for the 1975 |
| Time: | various | | | Canada Winter Games |
| Rating: | easy | | Maps: | 82G/8 Beaver Mines |
| Elevation gain: | negligible | | Note: | Motorized vehicles are |
| Mode of travel: | hike or ski | | | prohibited on these trails. |

## Overview and Comments

The Syncline cross-country trails system offers 15 km of looped trails and a chance for easy to moderate cross-country skiing, snowshoeing or an easy and relatively quick hiking option in the West Castle Valley. Developed for the 1975 Canada Winter Games and built on reclaimed logging roads, the trails work their way through rolling hills and a mix of lodgepole pine, poplar and open meadow.

There are trail maps available at the trailheads, but the best way to wend your way through the network is to review the maps posted at each trail junction. There are few amenities on these trails. Some benches are strategically placed to rest for a while, but there are no shelters or picnic tables. An Alberta government forest land-use zone designation prohibits motorized vehicles (other than the snow-packing machine) on the trails summer or winter, a welcome relief for those wanting to get away from the ATVs and snow machines which take over the Bow Crow Forest on summer and winter weekends. Unlike some other cross-country systems in the region, this one permits dogs, so occasionally you come across a dog team and sleigh or skijorers. This is not a skate-style venue, though; it is strictly for classic-style skiing.

Today a volunteer group, the Syncline-Castle Area Trail Association (or ScaT), maintains the trails, clearing brush in the off-season and packing them in winter. ScaT is slowly developing new trails which loop into the existing ones.

## Access

The trails are located on the road to the Castle Mountain Ski Resort, which is at the end of Highway 774. There are two trailheads, each with its own parking lot. The main lot is about halfway between the hamlet of Beaver Mines and the ski hill, a total distance of 14 km. The secondary lot is about 1 km before the main one. Both are on the east side of the road. (Leaving Beaver Mines, Highway 774 is paved and stays so for 8 km until it crosses the Castle River. After that, it is a well-maintained gravel road all the way to the ski hill.

## Exploring Beyond

Follow the cross-country ski trail along the lower slopes of the Westcastle Valley below Barnaby Ridge, from the Syncline Group Camp to the Westcastle Wetlands Ecological Reserve. This is mostly a leisurely walk through a rich riparian forest. Although the trail is close to the random camping areas along the Westcastle road, it remains a significant stretch of valley bottom that provides important habitat and movement corridors for wildlife.

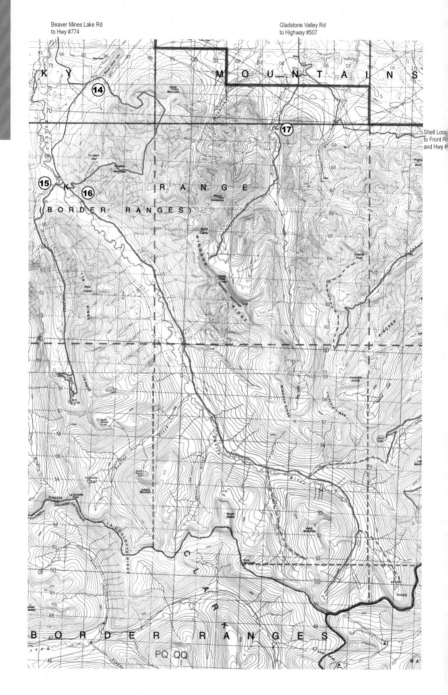

Beaver Mines Lake Rd
to Hwy #774

Gladstone Valley Rd
to Highway #507

Shell Loop
to Front R
and Hwy #

**La Coulotte Peak**

2438 m (8,000 ft.)

Located on the Continental Divide at the headwaters of the West Castle River and Roche Creek. Named after a First World War offensive by the 2nd and 3rd Canadian Divisions in April 1917 at La Coulotte, just outside Lens, France, near Vimy Ridge.

# South Castle Valley Hikes

## 14. TABLE MOUNTAIN – WHISTLER MOUNTAIN TRAVERSE

| | |
|---|---|
| Distance: | 4.5 km to Table Mountain summit; |
| | 12.5 km full traverse to South Castle road |
| Time: | 2.5 hrs. to Table Mountain summit; 8 hrs. for full traverse |
| Rating: | moderate to difficult |
| Start elevation: | 1465 m |
| Table Mtn. elevation: | 2150 m (false summit) 2230 m (actual summit) |
| High elevation: | 2275 m |
| Max. elevation gain: | 810 m |
| Terrain: | dirt forest trail, rock gully and open scree, open ridge, fire road |
| Mode of travel: | hike |
| Maps: | 82G/8 Beaver Mines |
| Note: | The traverse requires a car shuttle or a bike stashed at the end of the route. |

### Overview and Comments

While given separate names, Table and Whistler mountains are connected by a series of winding ridges and saddles. You can start the traverse from ei-

The sweep of Whistler Ridge offers views of Lys and Barnaby Ridges in the middle distance.

ther end, but the views as you hike southward are arguably more spectacular. Either way, the full traverse is a Castle classic. If you love hiking through varying ecotypes across long open ridges with sweeping vistas, this hike is worth the minor hassle of having to set up a shuttle at the trail's end. If you don't have a full day, the hike up Table Mountain is a worthy substitute.

The Castle Crown Wilderness Coalition leads an annual, late-summer, public hike along the classic Table-Whistle Traverser (www.ccwc.ab.ca).

**Access**

Drive 12 km south from Beaver Mines Highway 774 to the Beaver Mines Lake access road.

### to Trailhead:

Follow the Beaver Mines Lake access road into the campground, keeping to the right until you get to the signed trailhead. Park in the spaces provided.

### to Trail's End:

Take the Beaver Mines Lake road for 3.5 km and turn right on the South Castle road. Continue for 600 m until you get to a creek. You might have to make a decision, depending on the season. In early summer the creek is running and may be impassable with a regular vehicle. Later in the season the creek is dry and it is possible to drive across. After crossing, continue on the rough South Castle Valley road for 4.25 km until you cross a cattle guard. Look for a trail accessing the road from the east 750 m past the cattle guard. Park off to the side or stash your bike in the bush and drive back to trailhead in a second vehicle.

**Route Description**

### Table Mountain Summit:

A good clear trail starts you along, quickly passing through a gate before heading up through aspen forest. After 600 m you come to a lookout down onto the creek where you can see the debris stacked up by the 1995

The climb up the main gully offers the hiker a half-hour of cooling shade early on before the route hits the open slopes.

flood. Continue upward and cross a small footbridge. You then come to another viewpoint, looking across the drainage to a well-tracked slope and salt lick. Often, in the morning or late afternoon, mountain sheep come to replace minerals lost through the night or during the heat of the day.

From here the trail skirts back into the bush, detouring around a slump in the hillside. Once you are up on the open slopes, there are numerous trails leading upward, though not all of them may lead to the summit and often they end abruptly. The main trail turns to the right through a narrow but thick stand of dwarf pine and spruce and then opens onto a long traverse up the open slope heading to the large middle gully – the main route up Table.

Once at the base of the gully an obvious trail leads you 400 m up alongside a cascading mountain stream. Loose and wet rock can make footing tricky but it's not too bad. In the last 100 m the trail splits into numerous mini-routes, as users have sought the easiest ascent over the loose shale. Appreciate the cool shade of the gully while you can; once you are in the open there is very little cover the rest of the way.

Near the top of the gully, keep left, traversing a rocky slope 350 m up to the crest of a shoulder. Along the way you'll pass by and under some great old bone-white snags clinging to the red shale. The going is steep, but the shoulder offers a nice resting place before the final ascent up Table.

After you have climbed up and out of the gully a shoulder offers a resting spot and view of the peaks along the Continental Divide before the final push to the summit.

The final 500 m angles north from the shoulder, again traversing a steep, open rocky slope toward a sheer red cliff and what would appear to be the summit. But this is not the summit. Skirting to the east of the cliff and upon reaching the "top" you'll see why the mountain is called Table, with its wide plateau and precipitous 686 m drop straight down to Beaver Mines Lake. The real summit is another 1.5 km east along the ridge.

### Whistler Traverse:

Continue east along the ridge for 600 m as if you were going to the summit. Using the unique Castle Peaks of Windsor Mountain as a reference, begin to swing right, following a shoulder to a saddle between Table and Windsor. Stay high. Drop too low and you will have to bushwack through maze-like pockets of dense shrub to get to the saddle. Follow the shoulder down to where it levels off. Then, after cutting through the trees, ascend the opposite shoulder. Keep close to the edge for the easiest and most direct route. After 800 m you'll reach the high point of the hike (2275 m), the northeast peak on Whistler.

Once on Windsor Ridge, with its bright yellow and orange lichen-covered rock, you are quite exposed to the elements. Mountain avens, moss campion, saxifrage and other tufted alpine flowers are testimony to the potentially harsh conditions. But with exposure comes one of the most spectacular 360-degree panoramas in the Castle Wilderness.

After taking in the vista, continue south along the wide ridge, crossing on fractured mudrock and shale. Descend less than 500 m later off the ridge crest for another 100 m to avoid a cliff band, then continue on a traverse along the windward slope of the ridge, gradually ascending to another peak (2235 m). Exploring south around the peak to the shoulder brings excellent views of the Gladstone headwaters.

At this point head down and along a shoulder bearing east to west that leads toward an old fire lookout. Hike 500 m over bright red shale, passing oddly twisted snags of limber pine. Descend to a saddle and then climb again, following just below the ridge crest for a further 500 m. The ridge turns to the northwest for 400 m and then turns back west, dropping to an expansive flat below the fire lookout peak.

From this point the hike follows the abandoned fire lookout's old access road. Before dropping too low you can see Windsor Ridge and

Opposite top: Use the unique Castle Peak as a reference to access the rather unassuming saddle between Table and Whistler. Ascend Whistler Ridge along the edge of the trees.
Middle left: Views deep into the South Castle Valley from the old Whistler fire lookout road.
Middle right: Beginning the descent from Windsor Ridge along a shoulder that heads due west.
Below: View from highest point on the Table/Whistler Traverse. Prairie Bluff and Victoria Mountain are in the distance to the left, Windsor Mountain and its distinct Castle Peaks in the distant centre. The obvious triangular profile of Mount Haig is on the horizon to the far right.

213

far up the South Castle Valley: Spionkop, Newman's Peak, Avion Ridge and the square profile of Sage Mountain to the right. The last kilometre switches back down through open slopes of the small but ecologically significant Big Sagebrush Natural Area before entering a narrow section of forest at the trail's end.

### Table Mountain
2232 m (7,323 ft.)
Located southeast of Beaver Mines Lake and northwest of Gladstone Creek. Named in 1916 for the large plateau below the main the summit.

### Whistler Mountain
2210 m (7,250 ft.)
Located in the Castle River Valley at the head of Gladstone Creek. The mountain is named after the hoary marmot, also known as the whistling marmot.

## 15. GRIZZLY LAKE – RUBY LAKE

| | |
|---|---|
| Distance: | 11.5 km to Grizzly Lake, 12 km to Ruby Lake |
| Time: | 4.0+ hrs. to Grizzly Lake; 4.5+ hrs. to Ruby Lake |
| Rating: | moderate to difficult |
| Start elevation: | 1424 m |
| Low elevation: | 1389 m (South Castle crossing) |
| High elevation: | 2095 m (Ruby Lake overlook) |
| Ruby Lake elevation: | 2050 m |
| Grizzly Lake elevation: | 1930 m |
| Max. elevation gain: | 706 m |
| Terrain: | river and creek crossings, horse trail, single track, subalpine |
| Mode of travel: | hike, horseback |
| Maps: | 82G/8 Beaver Mines; 82G/1 Sage Creek |
| Notes: | Major ford of South Castle River and three crossings of Grizzly Creek. Popular with horseback riders; some ATV use. |

### Overview and Comments

A major ford of South Castle River is necessary. In late spring and early summer the water can be thigh- to waist-deep, cold and fast. Better to save this hike for later in the summer – July or August.

West shore of Grizzly Lake ...
... and Ruby Lake.

215

This hike takes you deep into the long, tight valley between Lys Ridge and Barnaby Ridge. Moderate to difficult because of its length and depending on the South Castle River, the route follows the valley bottom and lower benches for much of the way and is a test of patience. The payoff is two lakes: Grizzly, the larger of the two, is closer, but Ruby is the true gem. There is a wonderful camping area at Ruby Lake, surrounded by large fir, spruce and larch. Both lakes offer fishing.

Flooding in 1995 rerouted the lower section of Grizzly Creek.

**Access**

Drive 12 km south from Beaver Mines Highway 774 to the Beaver Mines Lake access road. Drive another 3.5 km and turn right (south) on the South Castle road. Follow for 600 m until you come to a creek crossing and a sign for South Castle road. Here you might have to make a decision depending on the season. In early summer the creek is running and may be impassable with a regular vehicle. Later in the summer the creek is dry and it is possible to drive across. After crossing continue south on the rough South Castle Valley road for 4.25 km until you cross a cattle guard. Park 1 km past the cattle guard and look for a well-used trail that heads over the side of the road and down to the South Castle River.

The last 6 km of the route follows along a bench below Lys Ridge; the first crossing of Grizzly Creek.

## Route Description

Follow this trail down to the river and cross. The South Castle can be thigh- to waist-deep, cold and fast in the early summer. Once across, looking back you can see the trail heading up Whistler Mountain (Page 207). The 1995 flood and subsequent spring flooding has played havoc with the original trail marked on old topographic maps. The old trail, which headed straight, paralleling Grizzly Creek, has been washed out. A recent route follows the new course of the creek. Pick up a trail on the west bank of the South Castle and veer left through trees and then straight along a gravel flood plain.

After 200 m, cross Grizzly Creek. After crossing, head straight through lodgepole forest. The trail turns south and climbs over a slight rise, actually the northernmost tip of Lys Ridge, before dropping gradually through thick alder to another ford of Grizzly. Follow for another 350 m to a fork. Go right, heading up the bench away from Grizzly Creek (left goes to a horse camp). After 350 m connect with the old, pre-flood trail and follow the bench. Once out of the forest cover, you get views of the steep-buttressed east wall of Barnaby Ridge.

After 1.25 km cross a major avalanche slope off Barnaby Ridge and drop down to Grizzly Creek. Cross the creek and ascend through a mix of forest and shrub to a bench. From here the trail follows the lower slopes of Lys Ridge for the next 3.5 km.

The first 1.75 km follows a cutline trail through alder and spruce, crossing numerous wet and dry streambeds. There are views above of West Castle peak, the highest point on Lys Ridge, the headwall above Grizzly Lake straight ahead, and Barnaby Ridge across the valley.

The trail then takes a slight dogleg to the right at the base of West Castle peak and crosses a stream before entering a short stretch of thick alder. Hike the next 1.5 km through sections of forest and shrub before emerging onto open bench. From here the trail becomes easier, crossing a section of scree and larger boulders before ascending slightly through a mix of open larch and spruce. As the trail levels off you can see Mount Haig over a low saddle on Barnaby Ridge.

217

Less than 2 km after crossing the scree slope (11 km into the hike) you come to a major fork in the trail. From here you have a couple of options.

### to Grizzly Lake:
Take the right-hand fork to Grizzly Lake. After 400 m, cross a creek and continue through trees for 1 km until you reach the north shore of Grizzly Lake. Camping is a little farther along the northwest shore.

### to Ruby Lake:
Stay straight at the fork and continue for less than 1 km until the trail veers down to a meadow. (Heading straight takes you to a dead end above Ruby Lake.) Once down in the meadow, follow the trail as it appears to head away from the lake. After 300 m, cross a creek and 150 m later you come to a junction. This is the trail coming up from Grizzly Lake. Turn left and follow a nice trail 500 m through alpine meadow to the north end of Ruby and a nice camping area.

### from Grizzly to Ruby:
It is possible to take a trail to Ruby from Grizzly. From the northeast corner of the lake, follow the most prominent trail heading up through the forest. There are a number of different routes. Follow the most-worn trail for 1.25 km until you come to a major fork. Stay straight for Ruby Lake.

### Lys Ridge
2522 m (8,274 ft.)
Located between Grizzly Creek and the Castle River Valley. The Lys River flows through Armentières, France. Named in 1917, likely in reference to Canadian troops during the First World War.

### West Castle Mountain
2316 m (7,600 ft.)
The highest point on Lys Ridge, West Castle Mountain lies across the Castle River far to the west of Castle Peak, one of the two high points on Windsor Mountain.

Meadow leading into Ruby Lake;
outfitter's campsite at Ruby Lake.

219

## 16. SOUTH CASTLE ROAD

| | |
|---|---|
| Distance: | 24 km |
| Time: | 4 hrs. |
| Rating: | moderate |
| Start elevation: | 1440 m |
| High elevation: | 1830 m |
| Max. elevation gain: | 390 m |
| Terrain: | dirt road |
| Mode of travel: | bike |
| Maps: | 82G/8 Beaver Mines; 82G/1 Sage Creek |
| Note: | On weekends there is fairly heavy use of off-road vehicles. |

The South Castle Road is the main access to the head of the South Castle Valley, where a number of remote trails and routes not documented in this book can be explored. The road is rough, but vehicles still use it from late spring into the fall. The route is long and at times monotonous. There are only a few minor climbs, making it very bikeable even for the novice.

Most washouts since the 1995 flood have been repaired. Still, depending on the time of year some fords may be necessary, especially near the head of the valley. The route can be wet and muddy early in the summer. Along the way there are numerous options, including the Whistler fire lookout, Grizzly Creek and the climb over the saddle to South Drywood Creek. The easiest route is to continue to the top of the valley and then hike up Avion Ridge, where you'll get wonderful views into Waterton Lakes National Park, or up the South Castle Divide, where the views are less spectacular. Because the road is relatively flat it takes about as long coming out of the South Castle Valley as it does going in.

**Access**

Take the Beaver Mines Lake road for 3.5 km and turn right on the South Castle road. Follow for 600 m until you get to a creek. You may have to make a decision here, depending on the season. In early summer the creek is running and may be impassable with a regular vehicle. Later in the season the creek is dry and it is possible to drive across. After crossing, continue on the rough South Castle Valley road for 4.25 km until you cross a cattle guard. Some 750 m past the cattle guard, look for a trail accessing the road from the east. Park off to the side and begin to bike from here.

## Exploring Beyond

There is a maze of trails, seismic lines and old logging tracks heading off the main South Castle road into the side drainages. Because they are not maintained they can be hard to find and it is harder to stay on track. Use the NTS topo map 82G/1 Sage Creek and be sure you are good at route finding.

### Font Mountain
2353 m (7,720 ft.)

Located on the Continental Divide in the Sage Creek Valley at the head of Font Creek. There is a font-like basin just to the west of this mountain.

### Sage Mountain
2368 m (7,769 ft.)

Located between Castle River and Font Creek. Named in 1916. The name likely refers to the sagebrush found in this fairly arid part of the Rockies.

### Jutland Mountain
2408 m (7,901 ft.)

Located between the headwaters of Jutland Brook and Scarpe Creek. Named in 1918, the mountain commemorates the Battle of Jutland, which was fought in 1916.

## 17. WINDSOR RIDGE

| | |
|---|---|
| Distance: | 7.8 km to lake |
| Time: | 3.5+ hrs. to lake |
| Rating: | moderate day hike or backpack |
| Start elevation: | 1485 m |
| Elevation at lake: | 2025 m |
| Max. elevation gain: | 520 m |
| Terrain: | creek crossings, horse trail, single track, forest benchland |
| Mode of travel: | hike; the first 2.5 km, to Mill Creek crossing, is bikeable |
| Maps: | 82G/8 Beaver Mines |
| Notes: | Major ford of Mill Creek; some minor route finding necessary. |

## Overview and Comments

Windsor Mountain is one of the most prominent landmarks in the Castle. Known as Queen Mountain by the Piikani, its distinct shape caught Thomas Blakiston's eye as he travelled the eastern edge of the Rockies in 1858:

> Looking to the mountains ahead of us I picked out the most prominent
> and took bearings on them. There were two near one another bearing
> thirty miles south, one of which, from the resemblance to a castle on its
> summit, I named Castle Mountain.

Blakiston's Palliser Expedition colleague James Hector, however, also laid claim to a Castle Mountain, in the Bow Valley west of Banff. In 1915, Blakiston's Castle was renamed Windsor Mountain because it resembled Windsor Castle in England. The Castle and North Castle remain the names of Windsor's two most prominent peaks.

There is good geological reason why Windsor Mountain is so prominent. The highest portion of the 10-km-long Windsor Ridge, which lies between Mill Creek and the Castle River Valley, the mountain is an island of harder Paleozoic rock within an area of softer, more readily eroded Precambrian shales, limestones and dolomites. (This erosion of sedimentary rock is partly why the Castle includes so many individual peaks but few higher

Approaching Windsor Mountain and its unique Castle Peak.

than 2500 metres.) The cliffs of Windsor Mountain resemble the Livingstone Range to the north more than its neighbouring peaks.

**Access**

*from Pincher Creek:*
Drive 15 km west of Pincher Creek on Highway 507 and turn left on the Gladstone Valley road. Follow this country road for 13 km, crossing Gladstone

Horse trail crossing avalanche path.

Creek and Mill Creek on the way. The profile of Windsor Mountain is visible for much of the way. Take the first right onto a well site road after crossing the bridge over Mill Creek. If you cross the cattle guard into the Forest Reserve you have gone 500 m too far. Drive 3 km to the end of the road and park in the open space south of the well site.

*from Highway 3/507 Junction:*
Drive south on 507 to Beaver Mines and continue on 507 east to Pincher Creek for 3.5 km. Turn right on the Gladstone Valley Road. For the rest of the directions, see the "from Pincher Creek" paragraph just above.

**Route Description**

Old topographic maps show the trail heading up alongside Mill Creek. Recent flooding has changed the course of the creek, and this early stage in the old route is now full of creek crossings. Instead, take the horse trail heading into the forest from the well site. This easy section passes south through forest and open meadows, eventually reconnecting with the old trail after 1.5 km. Continue south on this route for less than 1 km. Once you reach an open, gravel floodplain, begin looking across the creek for a trail cut through trees.

Cross the creek, which can be ankle- to knee-deep depending on the season, and pick up the trail on the opposite side. The first 150 m after the creek crossing is straight but the trail becomes less distinct as it crosses a series of gravel bars. Persevere for 200 m, picking up a trail passing through sections of trees. Look for a well-used horse trail on the north side of the dry creek. The trail, lined with thick alder, can get muddy. Ascend for the next 500 m, the first major elevation gain so far, and emerge onto an open bench with views of an unnamed ridge across the valley and the southeast face of Gladstone Mountain looming above. From here stay right and begin a steady ascent into the valley.

The next kilometre sees a series of avalanche paths with stream-cut gullies. Horseback riders have constructed a small corduroy platform to prevent the trail crossing the first gully from eroding away. After each avalanche path, the trail re-enters forest cover, finally emerging onto open bench above the creek. You can now clearly see Windsor Mountain and Castle Peak straight ahead.

Cross a washout and continue up alongside a narrow, boulder-strewn gully for 500 m, ascending to an open bench. From here, the trail is a leisurely pass through meadow and mixed conifer for 1 km, crossing a creek. From the crossing it is an easy 1 km to the lake. From the lake you have an unbroken 2 km view of Windsor Mountain's north face. Spend

some time to wander around the limestone boulders and crags on the lower talus slopes.

## Exploring Beyond

With its unique terrain, the Windsor Mountain basin offers some of the best exploring opportunities in the Castle. Traverse up scree below the north end of Windsor Mountain, skirting above trees to the saddle below North Castle peak. Explore the base of the peak or continue to Gladstone Mountain and a picturesque hanging valley above the Gladstone Creek headwaters. A more ambitious overnight exploration would be to follow the base of Windsor Mountain for 4 km from the lake, skirting around the east shoulder and into the next basin. From here it is possible to access the south end of Windsor Ridge and eventually onto a wide ridge above the Mill Creek headwaters. From here connect to Victoria Ridge above the Pincher Creek headwaters. (See the Pincher Creek/Victoria Ridge route, #18, page 227.)

### Castle Peak
2558 m (8,394 ft.)

### North Castle
2332 m (7,650 ft.)

Opposite: The small lake nestled at the base of the rockwall is one of the most secluded spots in the Castle, offering a the hiker a place to reflect on the future of the region.
Below: Windsor Ridge is an island of harder Paleozoic rock among the Castle region's softer, more readily eroded Precambrian shales, limestones and dolomites.

# Front Range Hikes

The Front Range is one of the truly remarkable areas of the Castle. Here, fescue grasses penetrate deeper into the mountains. Sprouting a month later than on the mixed-grass prairies, the fescues remain rich with nutrients late into the fall. In summers past as the grasses on the plains became parched and less nourishing, herds of bison would seek the lush buffet and welcome shelter of the native aspen groves in the Front Range valleys. In pursuit were any number of hunters, from the Stoney, Siksika, Piikani, Kainai or Ktunaxa nations, either sharing or vying for hunting territory. To go up any of the Front Range valleys is to seek a deeper connection to a landscape that a billion years ago was fresh and raw.

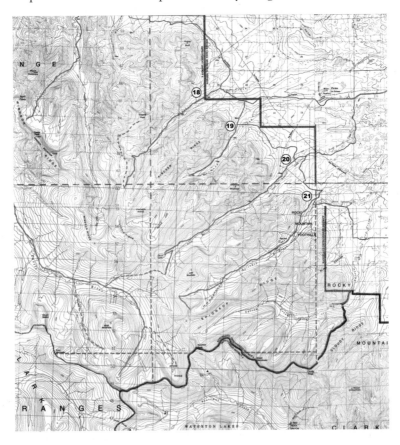

## 18. PINCHER CREEK – VICTORIA RIDGE

| | |
|---|---|
| Distance: | 8.75 km to ridge |
| Time: | 3+ hrs. one way (less if cycling first 4 km) |
| Rating: | moderate full-day hike |
| Start elevation: | 1540 m |
| High elevation: | 2225 m |
| Max. elevation gain: | 685 m |
| Terrain: | dirt road, double track, single track, subalpine, alpine |
| Mode of travel: | hike and/or bike |
| Maps: | 82G/8 Beaver Mines; 82G/1 Sage Creek |
| Notes: | The first 4 km follows a gated well site access road, and biking is recommended. From the ridge there is the option to summit Victoria Mountain or return along Pincher Ridge. |

### Overview and Comments

The most northerly of the Front Range hikes, this moderate day-long jaunt initially follows Pincher Creek through seasonally dry valley bottom and open benchlands, eventually ending up on the 10-km-long Victoria Ridge above Mill Creek Valley. The ridge offers the easiest route up Victoria Mountain, the highest peak on the Front Range but not the shortest. From atop the 2530 m (8,300 ft.) ridge you get a spectacular view of the east wall of Windsor Ridge.

### Access

Take Highway 6 south from Pincher Creek for 20 km. Turn west on Shell Plant Road and drive 14.5 km past the Shell-Waterton gas plant, ending up

Victoria Ridge looking toward Victoria Peak above the headwaters of Pincher Creek.

on a gravel road until you arrive at the Shell-Waterton Field Station. The road is gated at the Field Station. Park on the grassy area to the north.

**Route Description**

Enter the locked gate and walk or bike 3.75 km along the well site access road. Stay on the main road and where it ends at a well station take the double track passing through a small aspen stand. A running spring keeps parts of this section muddy. For next 2.5 km follow a trail along the north bench above Pincher Creek. Within the first 1.25 km there is a short side trail to a waterfall cascading off Victoria Peak, followed by a gravel bed washout and one ford of a mountain stream which can be almost dry by mid-summer.

After the ford climb slightly upward to a grassy meadow before coming to a major turn in the trail. The meadow can be soggy in early summer. Just as the trail bends to the right, a short side trail takes you down to a pleasant waterfall on Pincher Creek. This is a nice spot for a rest, since the main route is about to begin its first major ascent.

Instead of heading straight up the Pincher Creek Valley, which becomes narrow and heavily forested, the trail climbs up into a hanging side valley known locally as Thunder Basin. The ascent is moderately steep, first heading up alongside the creek flowing out of Thunder Basin and

Waterfall off the trail;
view back down the valley from Thunder Basin.

Scree slope exiting Thunder Basin.

then continuing through a series of switchbacks in the trees for 500 m, emerging onto an open slope of red shale. From this vantage point you can see back down the Pincher Creek valley. Head back into the trees once more for about 200 m. After crossing a creek, look for a major junction in the trail. At the junction take the left fork. Do not go straight unless you want to go deeper into Thunder Basin.

Quickly you are out of the trees and traversing a steep scree slope. At the end of the traverse you emerge onto a high, rocky bench overlooking Pincher Creek. From here the hiking eases along the open bench for 1.5 km, gradually climbing a series of ledges until reaching a sloped alpine meadow just before Victoria Ridge. From here it is a quick 500 m more to the ridge. Straight ahead you can see the headwaters of Pincher Creek. Pincher Ridge is across the valley. Once on the ridge you have a view of the east wall of Windsor Ridge and the Mill Creek valley below. The ridge can be very windy. A short ascent north on the ridge toward Victoria Mountain takes you to some interesting rock formations that are worth exploring.

# Exploring Beyond

### Victoria Mountain
2569 m (8,430 ft.)

To access the summit, follow the ridge heading northeast for 4.5 km. It is a pretty straightforward ridge hike, taking approximately one hour to reach the summit. En route you will skirt around the top of Thunder Basin. Choosing a route from the summit down into the Pincher Creek valley is less certain. Victoria has numerous cliff bands that need to be negotiated. If in doubt, head back along the ridge to Thunder Basin, descend the scree slope and pick up the main trail back.

### Pincher Ridge
2423 m (7,950 ft.)

It is possible to return via an 8 km ridge between Drywood Creek and Pincher Creek. Stay high along Victoria Ridge above the Pincher Creek headwaters and then follow the 8 km ridge. You'll have to negotiate a route down, which will mean bushwacking. The best option is to climb down a major side drainage 5 km along the ridge back into Pincher Creek valley.

### Prairie Bluff (Corner Mountain)
2254 m (7,395 ft.)

A secondary well site road 1.7 km from the gate is an easy, if less than spectacular, ascent. The summit does offer an impressive view of the surrounding rangeland (not to mention the Shell-Waterton gas processing plant, which dominates the vista). Named in 1941 because of its "bluff-like" profile, the peak is more commonly known as Corner Mountain.

### Victoria Ridge – Waterton Lakes National Park
The series of ridges at the end of each Front Range hike can be linked up, offering a wonderful two- to three-day hike to the northern boundary of Waterton Lakes National Park.

The extended hike from Victoria Ridge to Waterton Lakes National Park offers some of the most dramatic scenery in the Castle, seen here looking north from Spionkop Ridge.

## 19. NORTH DRYWOOD CREEK

| | |
|---|---|
| Distance: | 5 km to waterfall |
| Time: | 1+ hr. |
| Rating: | easy |
| Start elevation: | 1585 m |
| Waterfall elevation: | 1735 m |
| Max. elevation gain: | 150 m |
| Terrain: | gravel road |
| Travel mode: | hike or bike |
| Maps: | 82G/8 Beaver Mines; 82G/1 Sage Creek |
| Notes: | Road closed to motorized traffic except Shell Canada maintenance crews. There are remnants of a trail to the end of the valley, but expect to bushwack. |

### Overview and Comments

This is an easy but admittedly humdrum hike or short ride to a waterfall and swimming hole at the end of the North Drywood Creek well access road. Once at the end of the road it is a short walk on a worn trail to a rock outcrop and the 3-m-high falls.

Well site at the end of the road;
the waterfall is a short distance along a single-track trail.

Beyond the waterfall the double track that once led further into the valley has become overgrown and makes for an unpleasant bushwack. While it is certainly possible to follow the creek 4 km to the headwaters of Drywood Creek, or scramble up Pincher Ridge and continue to Victoria Ridge, other Front Range hikes are more suitable. Best to just enjoy the swimming hole and leave this valley to the wildlife.

## 20. SOUTH DRYWOOD CREEK

| | |
|---|---|
| Distance: | 9.5 km km to lake; 11.25 km to ridge |
| Time: | 3+ hrs. |
| Rating: | moderate |
| Starting elevation: | 1625 m |
| Lake elevation: | 2066 m |
| Ridge elevation: | 2230 m |
| Max. elevation gain: | 605 m |
| Terrain: | dirt road, double track, single track, subalpine, alpine |
| Travel mode: | hike and bike |
| Maps: | 82G/8 Beaver Mines; 82G/1 Sage Creek |
| Note: | First 4 km follows a well site access road that is popular with weekend ATV users. |

**Overview and Comments**

This is the only Front Range valley where the Castle Access Management Plan allows motorized use. ATVs, however, are not allowed at the lake or on the ridge. The saddle offers unobstructed views of some of the peaks deep in the Castle Wilderness: Sage and Font mountains and Mount Matkin. A trail continues down into the South Castle Valley.

Clockwise from top: panorama showing the trail to the ridge veering to the left
and the trail to the lake on the right;
berms and deadfall prevent ATV access to the lake;
trail drops down the last 150 m to the lake.

## Access

From Pincher Creek drive 20 km south on Highway 6. Turn west on Shell
Plant Road and drive 6.25 km. Before you get to the Shell-Waterton gas
plant, turn left onto Reviere Road and follow it into the Forestry Reserve.
Stay straight and continue to the South Drywood entrance. From the
open gate drive 4 km on the well access road. Park at the last well site.

## Route Description

Continue on a rough road heading out from the far northwest corner of
the well site. Most of the hike is up and down along open bench land with

views up hanging side valleys and cascades. After 2.5 km you come to a rocky ledge over South Drywood Creek with view of a waterfall farther up the valley. Cross a cattleguard 1.5 km later. From here the trail begins a steady ascent for 1.25 km to a large gravel pad.

From the gravel pad you can see the cutline up to the ridge. To get to the lake, continue on a rough makeshift trail for 500 m over a series of berms and piles of deadfall. These obstacles were built to discourage ATV use to the lake. Drop down into a small clearing just before the lake. Bovin Lake, or Blue Lake as it is sometime referred to, is about 400 m across at its widest. Stunted trees and shrubs at the east end of the lake offer cover from the wind and a good camping spot.

To access the saddle, return to the small clearing before the lake and follow an ATV trail for 500 m until it intersects the 1.5-km-long cutline to the ridge. Turn right. Small berms, stumps and deadfall dragged onto the trail clutter the lower section, again an attempt to prevent ATV use. After 250 m, cross a stream and begin the steady, sometimes steep ascent to the ridge. Along the way, you cross a larch meadow, and from there it is another 500 m of steady climbing to the ridge.

This ridge is part of the Victoria Ridge route to Waterton Lakes National Park (see page 230). An obvious trail runs the length of the

View from the ridge across South Castle Valley.
Left to right: Mount Matkin and Font and Sage mountains.

ridge and beyond, south to Loaf Mountain and north toward Victoria Mountain. From the ridge a well-used trail continues down the west side of the saddle into the South Castle Valley.

### Drywood Mountain

2514 m (8,250 ft.)

Located at the head of the valley between North Drywood Creek and South Drywood Creek.

### Loaf Mountain

2639 m (8,659 ft.)

Located between the headwaters of Spionkop Creek and South Drywood Creek. The mountain, one of the highest in the Castle, was thought to resemble a loaf of bread.

## 21. SPIONKOP

| | |
|---|---|
| Distance: | 10.5 km to ridge, 11.5 km to overlook, 10.4 km to subalpine lake |
| Time: | 3+ hrs. to ridge |
| Rating: | moderate to difficult |
| Start elevation: | 1520 m at locked gate; 1650 m at trailhead |
| Lake elevation: | 1830 m |
| Elevation above cirque: | 2260 m |
| Elevation at overlook: | 2420 m |
| Max. elevation gain: | 900 m |
| Terrain: | gravel road, double track, single track, subalpine, alpine |
| Mode of travel: | hike and bike |
| Maps: | 82G/8 Beaver Mines; 82G/1 Sage Creek |
| Notes: | First 4 km follows a well access road. Hike offers two options at the head of the valley: south basin or north cirque. The north cirque route to the ridge is the more popular. |

## Overview and Comments

Following the valley below the 8-km-long Spionkop Ridge to the south and Loaf mountain to the north, this hike is considered one of the finest in the Castle. The locked gate, a result of the Castle Access Management Plan, is helping the valley return to a less disturbed state. Unlike South Drywood drainage to the north (see page 232), which has ATV access, tall rough fescue and other native vegetation has returned to the bench above Spionkop Creek. As a result, much of the original trail is now nicely overgrown.

Hiking through untrammelled rough fescue is
a pleasure not found on many Castle routes.

The valley is bowl-shaped, and early into the hike you can see the panorama at the head of the valley. The valley eventually splits, offering two distinct hiking experiences. The tight valley tucked below Spionkop Ridge in the south basin, often referred to as Smith Canyon, holds two small but picturesque tarns. The route to the north is the most travelled and offers a sweeping cirque that leads to the ridge at the head of the valley. The ridge crest accesses some of the highest alpine terrain in the Castle: Loaf Mountain, 2639 m, and Spionkop Peak, 2576 m.

**Access**

From Pincher Creek drive 30 km south on Highway 6. Turn right (west) onto Spread Eagle Road and drive 8.25 km until you come to a

T intersection. Turn left (north) at the intersection and continue on the main road for 3 km, crossing a cattle guard into the Forest Reserve. Drive straight before dropping down and crossing a bridge over Spionkop Creek. Take the first left after the bridge and park off the road by the locked gate.

## Route Description

From the gate, bike or hike along the road, passing numerous well sites and flares as you climb to the trailhead. At 3.75 km a road veers left. Stay straight and come to a large gravel pad at 4 km, at the end of the road. Stash your bikes, if you cycled, and begin hiking. As with the other Front Range trails, you ascend onto open bench land above the creek. Spionkop early on is rich with vegetation and you're hiking on a trail lined with fescue, stickseed, geranium and clusters of small aspen stands.

Enter a spruce/fir stand. After 1 km, where an overgrown trail veers left, stay right and ascend onto a beautiful grassy meadow dotted with large boulders strewn from the upper cliffs of Loaf Mountain. The broad sweep of the valley continues to draw you in and the hiking is easy going for another kilometre, with spectacular views to the west of both the cirque to the left and Spionkop Peak to the right.

Gravel pad at trailhead. Loaf Mountain on the left, Spionkop to the right; trail heading into south basin.

Some 3.5 km from the trailhead you come to an overgrown fork in the trail. From this vantage point the south basin is to the southwest and the north cirque lies in the notch due west. Descend as if you are going to the south basin, and cross a stream flowing down from Loaf Montain. Just 100 m after crossing the creek, intersect a wide, well-worn trail and turn right up the valley toward the cliff separating the north and south routes. After re-entering some trees, you come to a junction in the trail.

To head into the south basin, keep straight, following the most prominent trails to the tarns. To head to the north cirque and ultimately the ridge top, take the right fork, which parallels the tributary flowing out from the north cirque. Follow this trail for nearly 1 km as it switches back through the trees, reaching a rocky bench, then continues ascending. The trail levels out and continues straight for 500 m through a pleasant subalpine meadow before ascending again up a slight headwall into the main cirque. Spionkop's north tributary offers an opportunity to refresh water bottles before climbing to the ridge crest. A snow cornice usually stays on the ridge crest late into the summer.

Once above the cirque, ascend the ridgeline south for 1 km to a notch at the base of Spionkop peak and a spectacular overlook above the tarns. Return via the same route.

### Spionkop Ridge
2576 m (8,453 ft.)
The ridge was named after Spion Kop Mountain in South Africa where a battle was waged during the Boer War. The eastern end of the ridge is referred to locally as Spread Eagle Mountain owing to its wingspread profile as seen from Highway 6.

Clockwise from top: Looking back down the cirque to the valley;
looking west from ridge into the South Castle Valley;
overlook above Smith Canyon.

239

# Recreation Activities

## Mountain Biking

Mountain biking along old logging and oil service roads is a recommended way to get to the trailheads of the gated Front Range canyons and to hikes deep into the South Castle and West Castle valleys or along the Lynx Creek Road. Overgrown and narrower or fragile trails in the montane, subalpine and alpine are best left to the hikers. Generally, most trails at lower elevations are rideable from May through October. Expect to get muddy early in the season, however. Also, rivers and streams can be high in May and June, and crossings can be hazardous.

In and of themselves, the South Castle River and West Castle River access roads offer long valley-bottom rides with enough creek crossings, ups and downs and views of surrounding ridges to make for a mildly interesting trip. If you like to slog up, get a view and then coast back down, try the Carbondale fire lookout road, or take the road past the locked gate to the top of Corner Mountain. For longer, technical rides of varying difficulty and over mountain passes, the North Kootenay/ MacDonald Creek and Middle Kootenay/Sunkist Ridge loops offer such opportunities. By linking either North Kootenay or Middle Kootenay pass with Akamina Pass through B.C.'s Akamina-Kishinena Recreation Area and returning via Waterton Lakes National Park, it is possible to do two- to four-day mountain-biking excursions.

(For full descriptions of mountain-biking trails, refer to Doug Eastcott's *Backcountry Biking in the Canadian Rockies*.)

## Horseback Riding

Trail riding is enjoyed year-round. Warm chinook winds throughout the winter can make winter riding quite pleasant. During May and into June the rivers and streams of the region run high and crossings can be difficult, if not impossible. Most rides along the valley floors are good novice trails.

Along ridges and open slopes, loose shale and switchbacks make riding more challenging and should only be attempted by experienced riders. Horse camping is allowed throughout the Forest Reserve, with proper permits. Weed-free feed is required.

## Rock Climbing

Because much of the rock in the southwestern Rockies is highly fractured and thus relatively unstable, there are no recommended climbs in the Castle.

## Caving

There are 14 known caves within a 4 km radius of the Crowsnest Pass, including: Yorkshire Pot, the third largest and second deepest in Canada; and Gargantua, the fourth largest and fourth deepest. The caves are primarily sinkholes channeled out by penetrating water over thousands of years. Most of the caves are found within the Mount McLaren, Mount Parrish, Mount Coulthard, Andy Good Peak grouping and reached via Ptolemy Creek outside the Castle boundary. Not all caves are accessible and route details are sketchy. It is dangerous to enter any cave without proper equipment and expertise! There are tour companies that offer trips into the caves.

## Canoeing and Kayaking

Paddling on the Castle River and Carbondale River is best in May and June, but often there is still enough volume in July.

### Castle River:
The Castle River from Highway 774 to Highway 3 is considered by many to be the most scenic, varied and challenging river in the region, with plenty of fun rapids from Class I to IV and an overall rating of

III. The section between Castle Falls and Highway 507 is the most challenging, with a continuous run of Class III+ to the confluence with the Carbondale River. The reach between the 507 and the Canyon bridge is Class II with good play spots. The bridge marks the start of the Castle Canyon. Surrounded by 40-m-high cliffs and with a series of difficult II+ to IV ledges, it should be attempted by experts. Portages: Castle Falls, Falls Rapids and the Castle Canyon.

| | |
|---|---|
| Rating: | III |
| Gradient: | 5 m/km (30 ft./mi.) |
| Season: | May through July |
| Discharge: | 23–70 m³/s (800–2,500 ft.³/sec.) |
| Velocity: | 5–8 km/h (3–5 m.p.h.) |

*Beaver Mines Lake:*
This small lake below Table Mountain is a pleasant morning or evening paddle but it can get very windy and choppy. The lake is ice free from mid-April until November.

# Winter Recreation

### Snow and Weather Conditions

Snowfall amounts in the region are variable. Snow accumulation can be quite low in the Front Range canyons, whereas in the alpine valleys along the Continental Divide snow pack can reach four metres. What snow does fall is usually dry snow. January and February are the coldest months and typically they have the most snowfall. Mean temperatures can range from –9° to –15°c. Temperatures can plunge to below –30°c.

Cold temperatures combined with dry snow forms a loose "depth hoar" that resists consolidating and is prone to avalanche. Chinooks occur frequently in the winter months, and these warm, dry winds can raise temperatures quickly, altering snow conditions considerably. Snow loading and wind slab on leeward slopes can be a problem, especially along the Continental Divide, where accumulation and winds are greatest. Avalanche conditions are typically unstable early in the winter before the snow pack has consolidated, and early in the spring when warm weather can create hazardous conditions.

Those travelling in the backcountry in winter should know not only the avalanche conditions beforehand, but how to test and assess snow pack, use avalanche safety equipment and perform avalanche rescue. The best local snow reports can be obtained from:

Waterton Lakes National Park
Warden Office: (403) 859-5140
Emergency: (403) 859-2636
24-hour recorded message: 1-800-667-1105
www.avalanche.ca

Castle Mountain Resort
www.castlemountainresort.com

**Winter Access**

Winter road access within the Castle is minimal. Highway 774 south of Beaver Mines is plowed to the Castle Mountain Resort and is the main road in. Well access roads into the Front Range canyons are also kept clear. Both the Adanac and Sartoris roads, accessing the Lynx Creek recreation area, are normally closed from November 31 to April 1 except for snowmobiles. Contact the Blairmore Forestry office for road updates.

**Cross-Country Skiing**

Syncline cross-country ski area, in the Castle Valley, is accessed by following Highway 774 for 15 km south of Beaver Mines. The area, originally developed for the 1975 Canada Winter Games, has a groomed trail network of 15 kilometres. Of the eight trails, six are rated novice, while the other two are blue-blazed intermediate trails.

## Ski Touring

The Castle is not widely known for ski touring. The best opportunities to explore the backcountry on skis can be found in the West Castle River valley, especially on the leeward slopes of Haig Ridge and up Middle Kootenay Pass. Haig, because of its proximity to the Castle Mountain Resort, is a well-known local backcountry haunt. The Front Range valleys offer some short, four-hour round trips, with access to some better snow farther back in the valleys. The roads into the Pincher, South Drywood and Spionkop trailheads are plowed to service the gas wells and it is often possible to bike the first 4 km. Snow pack can be thin and spotty along the trail because of the strong chinook winds, and some walking will likely be necessary. In some years it is possible to follow the creeks, where snow tends to drift in and accumulate.

## Ice Climbing

Because chinook winds can degrade ice very quickly, and because access to some of the major icefalls in the region is less than optimum, the Castle is not well known as an ice climbing destination. But the area's potential did not go unnoticed by Yvon Chouinard and others in the 1970s when a number of first ascents were made. The following descriptions are only basic guides to ice climbing in the Castle. Ice conditions vary considerably year to year.

## SOUTH DRYWOOD

(See South Drywood Creek trail description)

There are five climbs visible from the trail.

| | |
|---|---|
| Easter Bunny: | first drainage on south valley wall from trailhead; 100 m, grade 2. |
| Sunshine Corner: | second drainage south wall; scramble up west side of drainage; 90 m, grade 3. |
| Windy Corner: | continue 1 km from main trailhead; fall is on north side of valley; 45 m, grade 3, 75° to vertical ice. |

Two further climbs, The Drip and Slim Pickins, are short, grade 3 routes.


## NORTH DRYWOOD

(See North Drywood Creek trail description)

| | |
|---|---|
| The Gasser: | 75 m, grade 2, two-pitch climb on southeast side of valley. |
| Treading Water: | south face 40 m, grade 3 route; access 0.5 km farther up trail. |


## SOUTH CASTLE VALLEY

(See South Castle Road description)

Two advanced climbs accessed via 16 km of skiing and mountain biking up the South Castle road.

| | |
|---|---|
| Blue Angel: | southwest slope of Castle Peak; grade 4; 3 pitches; 1st 75° to 85°, 2nd 50° to vertical, final crux near vertical; Rappel route or descend west of route. |
| Lucifer: | 50 m west of Blue Angel; 90 m, grade 3; 2 long pitches on 70° to vertical ice. Rappel route. |

Route descriptions and grading derived from Joe Josephson's *Waterfall Ice*. The book is recommended for more detailed access, alpine and technical grading, and route and descent descriptions.

# Bibliography

Atwood, Wallace W. *The Rocky Mountains*. New York: Vanguard Press, 1945.

Beaty, Chester B. *The Landscapes of Southern Alberta: A Regional Geomorphology*. Lethbridge: University of Lethbridge Production Services, 1976, c1975.

Binnema, Theodore. *Common and Contested Ground: A Human and Environmental History of the Northwest Plains*. Toronto: University of Toronto Press, 2004.

"Brief History of the Canadian Pacific Railway, A." Montreal: CPR Archives, 2000–2002. Accessed Jan. 3, 2008, at www.cprheritage.com/history/display1.htm.

"Bringing it Back: A Restoration Framework for the Castle Wilderness." See Sheppard, David H. et al.

Bullchild, Percy. *The Sun Came Down: The History of the World as My Blackfeet Elders Told It*. San Francisco: Harper & Row, 1985.

Bustard, Bradley. *Pincher Creek: The Water, The Land, The People*. Pincher Creek, Alta.: Pincher Creek Watershed Group, 2005.

Clifford, Frank. *The Backbone of the World: A Portrait of the Vanishing West along the Continental Divide*. New York: Broadway Books, 2002.

"Crown of the Continent: Profile of a Treasured Landscape." Kalispell, Mont.: Crown of the Continent Ecosystem Education Consortium, n.d. Accessed as separate chapter PDFs Jan. 4, 2008, at www.crownofthecontinent.org/table_contents.htm.

Cruikshank, Julie. *Do Glaciers Listen? Local Knowledge, Colonial Encounters and Social Imagination*. Vancouver: University of British Columbia Press, 2005.

Cutler, Alan. *The Seashell on the Mountaintop: How Nicolaus Steno Solved an Ancient Mystery and Created the Science of the Earth*. New York: Plume, 2003.

Eastcott, Doug. *Backcountry Biking in the Canadian Rockies*. 3rd ed. Calgary: Rocky Mountain Books, 1999.

Elias, Peter Douglas. *From Grassland to Rockland: An Explorer's Guide to the Ecosystems of Southernmost Alberta*. Calgary: Rocky Mountain Books, 1999.

Ewers, John C. *The Blackfeet: Raiders on the Northwest Plains*. Norman, Okla.: University of Oklahoma Press, 1958.

Ferguson, Gary. *The Great Divide: A Biography of the Rocky Mountains*. Woodstock, Vt.: Countryman Press, 2006.

Fidler, Peter. "Journal of Exploration and Survey, 1789–1804." Hudson's Bay Co. Archives in the Archives of Manitoba, E3/2, fols. 106d-7.

Flores, Dan. *The Natural West: Environmental History in the Great Plains and Rocky Mountains*. Norman, Okla.: University of Oklahoma Press, 2001.

Foreman, Dave. *Rewilding North America: A Vision for Conservation in the 21st Century*. Washington, D.C.: Island Press, 2004.

Gadd, Ben. *Handbook of the Canadian Rockies*. 2nd ed. Jasper, Alta.: Corax Press, 1995.

Glenbow Museum, Blackfoot Gallery Committee. *Nitsitapiisinni: The Story of the Blackfoot People*. Toronto: Key Porter, 2001.

Grinnell, George Bird. *Blackfoot Lodge Tales*. Lincoln: University of Nebraska Press, 1962.

Hardy, W.G., ed. *Alberta: A Natural History*. Edmonton: M.G. Hurtig, 1967.

Heuer, Karsten. *Walking the Big Wild: From Yellowstone to the Yukon on the Grizzly Bear's Trail*. Toronto: McClelland & Stewart, 2002.

Jackson, John C. *The Piikani Blackfeet: A Culture Under Siege*. Missoula, Mont.: Mountain Press, 2000.

Jackson, Lionel E. Jr., & Michael C. Wilson, "The Ice-Free Corridor Revisited." *Geotimes*, February 2004. Accessed Nov. 23, 2007, at www.geotimes.org/feb04/feature_Revisited.html.

Jalkotzy, Martin. "Selected Ecological Resources of Alberta's Castle Carbondale: A Synopsis of Current Knowledge." Calgary: Arc Wildlife Services, 2005. Accessed Nov. 30, 2007, at www.cpawscalgary.org/campaigns_castle/pics/castle-carbondale-ecoresource-report.pdf.

Josephson, Joe. *Waterfall Ice: Climbs in the Canadian Rockies.* 4th ed. Calgary: Rocky Mountain Books, 2002.

Kennett, Steven A. "Integrated Resource Management in Alberta: Past, Present and Benchmarks for the Future," CIRL Occasional Paper #11, February 2002. Calgary: Canadian Institute of Resources Law. Accessed Nov. 30, 2007, at www.cirl.ca/pdf/OP11Benchmarks.pdf.

Kerouac, Jack. *The Dharma Bums.* New York: Viking, 1958. Reprinted New York: Penguin Books, 1976.

Kershaw, Linda, Andy MacKinnon & Jim Pojar. *Plants of the Rocky Mountains.* Edmonton: Lone Pine Publishing, 1998.

Kittredge, William. *Who Owns the West?* San Francisco: Mercury House, 1996.

Krech, Shepard III. *The Ecological Indian: Myth and History.* New York: W.W. Norton, 1999.

LaDow, Beth. *The Medicine Line: Life and Death on a North American Borderland.* New York: Routledge, 2001.

Lopez, Barry, & Deborah Gwartney, eds. *Home Ground: Language for an American Landscape.* San Antonio, Tex.: Trinity Press, 2006.

Lynx, Dustin. *Hiking Canada's Great Divide Trail.* Rev. ed. Calgary: Rocky Mountain Books, 2007.

Marty, Sid. *Leaning on the Wind: Under the Spell of the Great Chinook.* Toronto: HarperCollins, 1995.

Marty, Sid. *Sky Humour.* Windsor, Ont.: Black Moss Press, 1999.

McClintock, Walter. *The Old North Trail, or, Life, Legends and Religion of the Blackfeet Indians.* London: Macmillan & Co., 1910. Reprinted with introduction by S.J. Larson. Lincoln: University of Nebraska Press, Bison Books, 1992.

Most, Stephen. *River of Renewal: Myth and History in the Klamath Basin.* Portland: Oregon Historical Society Press in association with University of Washington Press, Seattle & London, 2006.

Nabhan, Gary Paul. *Cultures of Habitat: On Nature, Culture and Story.* Washington, D.C.: Counterpoint, 1997.

Ovid. *Metamorphoses.* Trans. Mary McInnes. London: Penguin, 1955.

Pincher Creek Historical Society. *Prairie Grass to Mountain Pass: History of the Pioneers of Pincher Creek and District.* Pincher Creek, Alta., 1974.

Potyondi, Barry. *Where the Rivers Meet: A History of the Upper Oldman River Basin to 1939.* Lethbridge: Robins Southern Printing, 1992 ["A Water Works publication"].

Pyne, Stephen J. *Fire: A Brief History.* Seattle: University of Washington Press, 2001.

"Ranching History." Canadian Encyclopedia online. Toronto: Historica Foundation, 2007. Accessed Nov. 24, 2007, at www. thecanadianencyclopedia.com/index.cfm?PgNm= TCE&Params=A1ARTA0006670.

Rand, Austin Loomer. *Mammals of the Eastern Rockies and Western Plains of Canada.* Ottawa: National Museum of Canada, 1948.

Robertson, Leslie. *Imagining Difference: Legend, Curse and Spectacle in a Canadian Mining Town.* Vancouver: University of British Columbia Press, 2005.

Ross, Jane, & William Tracy. *Hiking the Historic Crowsnest Pass.* Calgary: Rocky Mountain Books, 1992.

Russell, Andy. *Grizzly Country.* New York: Knopf, 1967.

Savage, Candace. *Prairie: A Natural History.* Vancouver: Greystone Books, 2004.

Sheppard, David H., Gary Parkstrom & Jennifer C. Taylor. "Bringing it Back: A Restoration Framework for the Castle Wilderness." Pincher Creek, Alta.: Castle-Crown Wilderness Coalition, 2002. Accessed Nov. 28, 2007, at www.ccwc.ab.ca/ccwcbref/ReportsandDocs.html/ BRINGING_IT_BACK.pdf.

Solnit, Rebecca. *Wanderlust: A History of Walking.* New York: Penguin, 2000.

Southwest Alberta Recreational Trail Map. Pincher Creek, Alta.: Southwest Alberta Business Development Centre, 1995.

Spry, Irene M. *The Palliser Expedition: The Dramatic Story of Western Canadian Exploration 1857–1860.* 2nd ed. Saskatoon: Fifth House, 1995. Originally published Toronto: Macmillan, 1963.

Turner, Frederick W. *Beyond Geography: The Western Spirit against the Wilderness.* New Brunswick, N.J.: Rutgers University Press, 1992.

Tweedie, James. "Why We Hike." *Castle Wilderness News* 17(3), August 2007. Pincher Creek, Alta.: Castle-Crown Wilderness Coalition. Accessed Nov. 28, 2007, at www.ccwc.ab.ca/ccwcbref/Newsletters.html/CastleNewsAug07.pdf.

Urquhart, Ian T., ed. *Assault on the Rockies: Environmental Controversies in Alberta.* Edmonton: Rowan Books, 1998.

Waldt, Ralph. *Crown of the Continent: The Last Great Wilderness of the Rocky Mountains.* Helena, Mont.: Riverbend, 2004.

Walton, Dawn. "Were bison one of globalization's first victims?" *The Globe and Mail*, July 31, 2007, A3.

Warhus, Mark. *Another America: Native American Maps and the History of Our Land.* New York: St. Martin's Press, 1997.

Weide, Bruce. *Trail of the Great Bear.* Helena, Mont.: Falcon Press 1992.

Worster, Donald. *The Wealth of Nature: Environmental History and the Ecological Imagination.* New York: Oxford University Press, 1993.

## Government documents

Alberta Energy & Natural Resources, Public Lands & Wildlife Division. "A Policy for Resource Management of the Eastern Slopes, Revised 1984."

Alberta Natural Resources Conservation Board. "Vacation Alberta Corporation Expansion of Existing Recreational and Tourism Facility in Pincher Creek Area – Application No. 9201: Report on Pre-Hearing, March 30, 1993."

Alberta Natural Resources Conservation Board. "Vacation Alberta Corporation Expansion of Existing Recreational and Tourism Facility in Pincher Creek Area – Application No. 9201: Final Report, December 1993."

Waterton Lakes National Park/Canadian Heritage/Parks Canada. "Waterton Resource Guide." 1997.

## Websites

Alberta Wilderness Association: www.albertawilderness.ca

Canadian Parks & Wilderness Society, Calgary/Banff Chapter: www.cpawscalgary.org

Castle Crown Wilderness Coalition: www.ccwc.ab.ca

Cows and Fish: www.cowsandfish.org

Crown of the Continent Ecosystem Education Consortium: www.crownofthecontinent.org/coceec.htm

Glacier National Park: www.nps.gov/glac

History of the Crowsnest Pass Highway: www.crowsnest-highway.ca

Ktunaxa Nation: www.ktunaxa.org

Nature Conservancy of Canada: www.nature.org/wherewework/northamerica/canada

Southern Alberta Land Trust Society: www.salts-landtrust.org

Treaty Seven Management Corp.: www.treaty7.org

Waterton Lakes National Park: www.pc.gc.ca/pn-np/ab/waterton

# Index

## About the Author

Robert Kershaw is a communications consultant, writer and photographer. After graduating from the University of Calgary with a Bachelor of Science in Ecology and Communications Studies, Rob moved to Pincher Creek, where he worked as a ranch hand and co-owned a small communications company that published the *Waterton-Glacier Views*, a weekly newspaper concerned with community development, conservation and environmental issues. Rob is presently living in California with his wife, Emily Paulos, where he is Director of Canadian Projects and a teaching associate with the Center for Digital Storytelling in Berkeley.